Can a gorgeous, shy, athletic model from Texas find happiness with a strapping six-foot ex-football player from Kentucky?

You better believe it when the couple is Farrah Fawcett and Lee Majors—
The Bionic Man and his Angel!

Farrah & Lee

by Connie Berman

tempo
books

GROSSET & DUNLAP
A FILMWAYS COMPANY
Publishers • New York

PICTURE CREDITS: United Press International, pages 47, 110 (top); Phil Roach-Photoreporters, pages 48, 50 (bottom), 51, 107, 111; Photoreporters, page 110 (bottom); MC Broom-Globe Photos, page 49; Globe Photos, page 109; Frank Edwards-Fotos International, pages 50 (top), 108; Pictorial Parade, page 52; Wide World Photos, page 112.

Farrah & Lee
Copyright © 1977 Connie Berman
All rights reserved
Published simultaneously in Canada
ISBN: 0-448-14275-9
A Tempo Books Original
Tempo Books is registered in the U.S. Patent Office
Printed in the United States of America

Farrah & Lee

Forget about Paul Newman and Joanne Woodward. And forget about Clark Gable and Carole Lombard. Even Sonny and Cher can't compete with Hollywood's newest and most exciting couple of the decade—Lee Majors and Farrah Fawcett.

She's sexy and with-it and beautiful, with a gorgeous, burnished mane of hair and an ear-to-ear grin of pearly white perfect teeth. He's handsome, athletic and brawny, a real man's man kind of guy. If any couple could be perfectly matched by computers, it would have to be Lee Majors and his breathtakingly stunning wife, Farrah Fawcett-Majors.

Together they reign as king and queen of the television air waves. Lee's the star of "The Six Million Dollar Man," a science fiction–inspired series about a bionic being, a combination of human and machine. Aided by his electronic parts, Lee thwarts criminals with his superhuman talents. Farrah's methods of dealing with law and order on "Charlie's Angels" are much more down to earth. She uses her feminine wiles and the police skills she learned along with her partners, Kate Jackson and Jaclyn Smith.

Things have changed quite a bit in the Majors household in the past year. It used to be that Lee was the big-name TV star, and although Farrah had an easily recognizable face from her hundreds of television commercials, no one knew who she was. Now something called the Farrah craze is sweeping the country. She's America's newest and most-beloved sweetheart. Everybody loves Farrah. Men swoon over her looks, and women admire her and respect her. She was voted the most-admired personality by a group of teens. A pin-up poster of her in a one-piece bathing suit has emerged as the hottest-selling poster of all time, numbering more buyers than pin-ups of Marilyn Monroe or Betty Grable, or even the fabulous Fonz.

And it all happened as a result of her work on "Charlie's Angels." Before that, Farrah was a traffic-stopping face but not a celebrity. Now that the ABC series has planted itself very solidly in top-ten Nielsen territory week after week, Farrah's one of the most-watched and best-known actresses in the country. She's so famous now that just her first name is enough. Just like Cher, Liz, and Jackie, everybody knows who Farrah is.

Yet the fame and adulation, the fact that hordes of fans recently stampeded a California magazine office when they learned that Farrah Fawcett was to be cover girl and cover story, have hardly gone to her feathery-tressed head. What she really likes best out of life is her marriage to Lee and the simple domestic chores she performs, gladly, for him—like making dinner and baking cookies.

And she laments the fact that three of her favorite activities—grocery shopping, movie going, and clothes shopping—have been severely curtailed by her sudden stardom. She can't indulge as freely as she'd like in these cherished pastimes unless she wants to while away her free time signing autographs by the dozens.

The comparisons between Farrah and that other blond actress, Marilyn Monroe, bewilder and bother her a bit. She is, after all, quite blissfully married and content to spend the rest of her days with just one man—her husband Lee.

Farrah's rise to stardom may be the stuff that Hollywood scripts are made of, but her life with Lee is not grist for the gossip mill, like some other stars' lives—Liz and Cher, for instance. And neither, for that matter, is Lee's. A reserved, low-key type of guy, who enjoys evenings alone with Farrah and time in the woods or out on a lake fishing, with just her around, Lee is not your typical Hollywood matinee idol. He'd much rather talk about his pretty wife than he would discuss his own abilities and career. Rather than play the jealous husband, anxious about the neck-and-neck competition in her television career, Lee is frankly quite proud of his wife's success and seems to enjoy all the attention she's getting. You can look high and low for snags in the Fawcett-Majors marriage, but there just aren't any.

Perhaps the fact that their relationship is such a close one, that their egos have hardly expanded with the growth of their popularity, can be laid down to their achieving stardom almost by accident. Neither of them was driven to become a great celebrity. It was a case of serendipity. Lee headed out to California, intending to become a teacher and a football coach (but with the idea of becoming an actor in the back of his mind), and after a few years wound up in acting. Farrah came out to Hollywood on a lark, lured by offers from publicity agents but convinced that nothing much was going to happen. When it all did, she was surprised. She still can't believe that she's the object of such ardent affection of millions of people all over the country.

While Farrah is scaling the heights of stardom with her very first series, Lee's position as a front-liner on TV goes way back to the days when he played the son Heath on "The Big Valley" with Barbara Stanwyck. Since then there have been "The Men from Shiloh" and "Owen Marshall," but only with "The Six Million Dollar Man" has he achieved top billing and full star ranking. To boot, he's become as much of a cult hero as his wife. He's regarded as a kind of superman hero, a modern-day knight in bionic disguise. In these times of gun-toting gangsters and fist-brandishing revolutionaries, Lee is an old-fashioned guy who is the champion of right over wrong.

Physically Lee and Farrah have all the credentials it takes to be top screen idols in America. But when it comes to personalities, they're hardly into the star syndrome. They could probably afford a much more lavish home than their current French-provincial residence in Bel Air, but they wouldn't want to move. They like it there and it's cozy and right for their life-style. Lee couldn't care less about clothes, and he is happiest when he's pursuing one of his favorite sports—like football, golf, fishing, hunting, tennis. Farrah is untroubled by the usual star handicaps. She loves her life and had a painless childhood and is traditional enough to still practice her religion. Neither of them spend time on an analyst's couch. But for the fact that they happen to be Farrah and Lee, two of TV's hottest stars, they could just be girl-next-door and boy-next-door, happily united in matrimony. With the crowds cheering for her and the sacks of fan mail pouring in, Farrah exclaims, "I like my marriage and him being the most important thing in my life."

It is rumored that despite Farrah's consciousness of her mushrooming popularity and her desire to get into films, she wants to leave "Charlie's Angels" to be able to spend more time with her husband. And working so hard on a weekly series every day is not her idea of great fun. Like the Southern belle she is, Farrah likes to enjoy life, and a lot of that enjoyment comes from spending time with her husband.

Neither Lee nor Farrah would sell their souls for fame. They're well aware that stardom can be fleeting, but if their celebrity should pass, it won't be the end of the world for them. Farrah thinks that good things are in store for her, like big movie roles and more important projects, but if none of this should happen, it won't destroy her. By the same token, Lee, who has watched his wife rise to become one of the hottest commodities in Hollywood, feels that if her fame should eclipse his, he'd be content to just sit back and bask in her glory. Stardom is something that has been described by both of them as "nice"; but it's certainly not the be-all and end-all of their lives.

And yet, despite their easygoing attitudes, and their refusals to fight and drive for the top, the offers for Lee and Farrah are pouring in. They can remain as unruffled by their popularity as they like, but the forces that be in Hollywood are certainly going to bombard them with offers. After all, when a girl sells more than two million copies of a poster there's obviously a tremendous star potential there.

Yes, things are changing rapidly in the Majors household. The pressure is hot and heavy, and the attention is overpowering. The money talk is incredible and the whole world seems like a dream. But that's the way it is when you become a star. Lee Majors knows what it's like—now Farrah is rapidly acquiring that terrible yet exhilarating knowledge of stardom.

No wonder she says, with her wide-eyed, flashing beauty, "I have a feeling that in this life, at this particular time for me, everything's being taken care of for me . . . and I've been very blessed."

_____ **2**

When Lee Majors was barely into his teens, he made a startling discovery that would affect his life and dramatically shape his thinking for the rest of his days. It was a discovery that in large part explains his burning desire to succeed as an actor and his fervent dedication to doing well and reaching the top of his profession. In a way, that discovery explains why Lee is the famous star he is today, and not just another struggling actor doing bit parts between stints on the unemployment line.

It was a wet, rainy afternoon in Middlesboro, Kentucky, about twenty-five years ago. Lee was then a tall and husky youth of thirteen, remarkably well developed for his age, with a shock of thick blond hair. Usually the athletic boy played football or baseball with his friends, but he and his pals could do nothing outside on a nasty day like this. With all the typical restlessness of an energetic teenager cooped up inside, Lee was bored and fidgety. After pacing through the house, he decided to explore.

His choice for an exploration site was the attic of his family's home, a musty, dust-covered place filled with old books, old clothes, big boxes, and crates. It was not as much fun as winding up on the pitcher's mound, but it would be interesting to rummage through the boxes to see what relics from the past he could find.

And that was when Lee learned something about his own past that shocked him. He unfastened the lock on an old trunk and was flipping through some old newspaper clippings. Suddenly he sat bold upright as the contents of one of them revealed to him an amazing truth about his identity. Lee was not the child of the two wonderful people he called mother and dad, the kindly couple that he loved more than anything else in the world. His own parents were dead. Lee was adopted!

"That's when I learned that my father had been killed at the steel mill where he worked while my mother was pregnant with me. And I found out that when I was two, my mother was struck by a car and killed," Lee recalls.

It was a rude shock for the young boy. So many new and staggering facts to deal with at once. His thoughts were confused, bewildered, muddied. It was desolating to discover and understand that he was not the natural child of the people with whom he had lived for so many years. It was even more of a stunning blow to realize that both his parents had been killed, his own father dead before Lee was even born. Not once, even as a newborn baby, had he seen his own father.

Lee had been brought into this world on April 23, 1939, in a suburb of Detroit called Wyandotte, the son of a woman who was already a widow. And then, when he was still just a baby really, his mother had died. His aunt and uncle, Harvey and Mildred Yeary, had adopted him and welcomed him into their home in the hill country of Middlesboro, Kentucky, as one of their own. His adoptive parents had raised him from that time on. Lee, whose real name was Harvey Lee Yeary, had been too young to realize what was happening—that he had been left motherless and fatherless and was moving all the way from Michigan to Kentucky to live with new parents.

But now, all these facts filled his teenage head as he clutched the newspaper clippings that told about the early and tragic deaths of his natural father and mother. All sorts of strange and different thoughts clouded his mind. His imagination ran wild with thoughts of what being adopted really meant.

Lee felt perplexed about the boy he had regarded as his brother until this moment. The boy, who was five years older than Lee, had bossed him around, as all senior siblings will. They like to show the younger brother the ropes, and yet at the same time they feel the need to exert their authority by dint of their years. Lee now felt resentful about his brother's bossiness. He realized that the older boy wasn't really his brother after all, if he had been adopted. But one thing about his older so-called brother inspired him. The lad was a terrific athlete. Lee resolved to try his best to become an even better one.

Lee was determined to be the best he could in everything. He set out from that rainy day in his family's attic to prove to others—but mostly to himself—that he was worthy. He felt that he had to show his stepparents that he was deserving of the choice they had made. After all, they didn't have to take Lee in after his own parents had died. He could have been brought up in a foster home or an orphanage. Lee felt tormented by pangs of guilt at the sacrifices his stepfather and stepmother had made in his behalf. And, he kept thinking over and over, he wasn't even their real son. They had done so much for someone who was not their natural child.

"I made up my mind right then that my stepparents would never regret having adopted me," he remembers. "I set out to prove myself."

Lee felt doubly obligated to prove himself worthy and to repay his stepparents for having raised him because he knew what hardships they had undergone to provide for him. The Yearys were far from rich; in fact, most of the section where Lee grew up he later described as completely poverty-stricken. It was backwoods country, where there was a lot of moonshine and hillbilly music.

"Kentucky is the number-one producer of bourbon in the country, but eighty-five of its counties are dry. My county was dry, but it had so many bootleggers they wore black armbands to keep from selling to each other. . . . The town is so small, we have an all-night diner which closes at two in the afternoon," jests Lee.

But Lee was dedicated to rising above his surroundings. He demonstrated his ability to excel through his prowess in sports. It wasn't enough for Lee merely to be good at athletics—he had to be the best! He had been an indifferent, not very noteworthy football player, but Lee set out to change all that. He decided that he would gain recognition and attention by being proficient with the pigskin. He quickly became the star of his high school football team, armored with the drive and single-mindedness that would characterize his rise to stardom later in life. Awards and citations began to come his way. He was named a member of the Kentucky All-State football team. When it came time for Lee to graduate from high school and go on to college, the sports hero had a number of offers tendered his way. He finally settled on the University of Indiana, which he attended on an athletic scholarship.

"I played football at the University of Indiana on a scholarship," remembers Lee. "I was supposed to go to Kentucky University when I got the Indiana offer. . . ." Then he transferred to the University of Eastern Kentucky and finished up there with a degree in Education.

His friends in college recall Lee as a talented, gifted athlete, but one who was driven to succeed and to win. They describe him as being upset by a lost game or a mishandled pass during a football game, someone who took each forfeited point very hard. He had the kind of killer instinct that separates the great athletes from the merely good ones. The athletes who want to win so badly that in the end they will—the ones whose determination in fact carries them on to victory. For Lee, even a football game or a basketball match was simply not a contest between two teams. It was more than that. It was a test of life—it was a chance and an opportunity to prove himself.

It seemed inevitable that Lee would join the ranks of the professional sports world after college. Scouts from various pro teams had noticed the youth had the kind of drive that would catapult him into the Hall of Fame. But tragedy stepped in and thwarted Lee's chances to go pro. During one game, Lee was tackled so hard and furiously by a member of the opposing team that the next day he was rushed to the hospital.

He recalled the shock when, the morning after the game, "I woke up paralyzed from the waist down." Terrified, Lee was taken to the hospital immediately. His fears about his legs were not dispelled right away. Instead, his anguish deepened when he heard the doctors tell him that there was doubt whether he would be able to walk again. Lee had been worried that he might not be able to finish the football season. Now the doctors confronted him with something much worse—the possibility that he would spend the rest of his life in a wheelchair!

Lee's injury was aggravated by the fact that, previously, unknown to him or anyone else, he had been suffering from a defect in his spine. The defect resulted in a condition known as spondylolisthesis.

Like faith healers who ignore the most dire diagnoses and cure the most crippling illnesses, Lee didn't care what the doctors thought or said. He had to walk again. He was not going to be a cripple for the rest of his life. He was determined to get up out of his hospital bed—to take steps, to walk.

More than that, he knew he was going to play football

again. Once more, the urge to prove himself, to battle the odds, overwhelming as they may be, swelled inside him.

Lee spent about a month in the hospital. Much to the amazement of the physicians who were treating him, he was able to stand up after two weeks. Before that, he had barely been able to move in his hospital bed.

"I was paralyzed for two weeks," Lee says, his voice a somber recollection of that painful time. "I was really frightened."

Once he found that he could stand up, Lee struggled to regain his balance and control so that he could walk again. Soon he was making such good progress that he was able to return to school. Football, according to the stern advice of his doctors, was definitely out. His doctors warned him that if he ever played again, he would risk the chance of crippling injury, and that the next time the outcome might not be so positive.

But he had once triumphed over the doctors' gloomy predictions, so Lee felt in his heart that if he wanted to, he could play football and not be injured. The next year he was back at his old position on the Eastern Kentucky State College team, pursuing the pigskin.

To the fans in the stadium, Lee was in as fine shape as ever, but he knew that the injury had left its mark. He felt that he wasn't as competent a player as he had been before the injury. He felt that his reflex time was slower, and he found himself not so willing to take chances in the game.

But Lee was still playing in championship form. He was doing so well that upon graduation from college, he received an offer to go professional with the St. Louis Cardinals in the National Football League. He mulled the proposition over in his mind and turned it down. His doctors had advised him against it, but there were other considerations. Lee wanted to be a great professional football player, but he felt that his injury would hinder him, that it would prevent him from playing the kind of ball he wanted to.

Instead, Lee began to formulate other plans for his future. He had graduated with enough education credentials to teach school, and he considered combining a teaching career with a coaching job. If he wouldn't be playing professional football himself, he could at least inspire other boys to the kind of gridiron greatness he admired.

But there was something else lurking in the back of his mind. Lee was toying with the idea of another field that would give him the same kind of national recognition and worldwide attention he would have reaped from a great football career. That field was acting.

When Lee told his friends about his fantasy of becoming an actor, they were stunned. It was a very uncommon thing for a youth from Kentucky to do. After all, it wasn't as though he had been raised in California, surrounded by the movie and television industry, walking the streets with famous stars, breathing in the almost supernatural aura given off by the celebrities of Hollywood. Kentuckians may have become football heroes, but show business was out of their ken.

But not for Lee. From the beginning he was inspired by the same kind of drive that propelled him onto the football field. He didn't want to become a bit part actor scrounging for parts and worrying where his next rent check would come from. He wanted to do well. When his pals reacted dubiously about his chances in Hollywood, Lee would reply: "I'm going to make it. . . . I've got to!"

And so the well-built, good-looking ex-jock came to Los Angeles in 1959, the town where stardom becomes a reality for a few of the citizens and continues to remain a far-off dream for many others. Lee landed a job as a recreation director for the Los Angeles Department of Parks and Recreation at North Hollywood Park. The job paid a paltry $2.83 an hour, but Lee was glad to be employed and continued to nurse his acting dreams.

Like most places in Hollywood, this park was not just a simple park; it was also affected by the glitter and the glamour of the show business world around it. It even had its own special roster of star graduates, such as the late movie actor Alan Ladd, who had once worked there as a lifeguard.

Many of the people Lee encountered in the park, especially during his informal games of touch football, were connected with show business. Many of them were men like himself—not better-looking, or shrewder. Lee began to realize that becoming an actor was not out of his realm, but quite within possibility. After countless bull sessions with these other young hopefuls of the acting world, Lee chucked his plans to become a football coach once and for all. "I decided to try it," he says.

With no idea of how to go about getting into acting, Lee mustered his courage and presented himself, without any introduction, at the office of Dick Clayton, one of the top Hollywood agents. He brashly talked his way into seeing

Clayton, getting past those formidable secretaries agents are infamous for. Clayton, who handled some of the biggest names in Hollywood and no unknowns, was nevertheless impressed with Lee. He felt that there was potential in this rough-hewn young man from Kentucky with the thick drawl. But he was chagrined at the fact that this guy who said he wanted to be an actor had no serious acting experience. He had been too busy playing football and basketball in college to take things like dramatic classes. Clayton suggested that Lee find a good drama coach and begin studying the craft.

The new boy in town from Kentucky did just that. He went to see Estelle Harmon, one of Hollywood's most respected drama coaches, and enrolled in her classes for intense acting study.

Harmon remembers that Lee was terribly earnest about becoming an actor—it wasn't a case of an idle fancy to him. She also felt that at times his husky good looks hampered him, that people tended to react to him simply as a handsome jock, instead of a talented actor. She also recalls that he was very sensitive and quiet, and nervous about making a mistake or looking silly or awkward. He yearned, she has said, to be taken seriously.

After about a year of study, Lee again returned to the plush offices of Clayton. This time he was accompanied by a pretty young actress. Lee wanted to do a scene for Clayton, to demonstrate to the agent how much he had learned, how much he had developed in the year he had been taking courses.

"You're coming along," remarked Clayton favorably, after Lee had done his bit of acting with the young starlet. He then chatted with Clayton, who promptly invited him to come along while the agent talked to some people on the studio lot at MGM. That trip was a fortuitous one for Lee. When Clayton introduced Lee to an MGM executive, the executive asked Majors (as he was then known around Hollywood), if he would like to train with the studio contract players.

After a few months with the MGM contract players, Lee was chafing at the bit. He wanted a professional part, even if it was only a few lines—or no lines at all. He had been studying all this time and was anxious to land a real role. He saw many of his classmates getting jobs and envied them. So again he sought out Clayton, who was by this time Lee's self-appointed guardian angel in Hollywood, and asked him to help him get a part.

But Clayton demurred. He felt that Lee should wait for the right part at the right time. He felt that it was a matter of the proper exposure for Lee; if the fledgling actor made his debut in a mediocre role, he could be finished before he even started. So he discouraged Lee and instead suggested "If you want bit parts, I'd be glad to recommend an agent who goes in for that sort of thing."

Lee got the message. He decided that Clayton knew more about the business than he did and he opted for trusting his agent's opinion.

After a full six months' of training with MGM, Lee again showed up at Clayton's office to perform another dramatic scene. Clayton was not only excited about Lee's ability, he was also convinced that the husky actor was ready to make his debut.

"You're ready," he told Lee. With that comment, he escorted a rather surprised Lee to the producers of "The Big Valley," a new series. The producers were looking for three good-looking men to play the sons of a widowed ranch owner. Lee was signed up for his very first interview.

It was to be the first of many interviews for Lee. There were also a series of screen tests he had to go through. It was certainly a tense situation for Lee, considering that he was pacing through all these procedures for the first time.

The competition was stiff. After all, Lee was a newcomer, trying out for his very first professional role. There were some 400 other actors who were reading for the part of Heath Barkley. Many of them were well-seasoned veterans of the acting business with long lists of credits behind them. Some of them had even established reputations for themselves.

"They asked for my credits," Lee remembers, "and I didn't have any." He confesses that he was "very scared and nervous" because he was contesting with so many other actors who were far more experienced.

But Lee's determination and ability won out in the end. Although he had never worked professionally before, he won the coveted role of Heath and was set to act in the pilot.

Lee was gratified that his devoted study and his patience had been rewarded. He was also pleased that his basic self-confidence had helped him to win out over so many other actors. His first role was a plum—a major one. But Lee wasn't self-confident to the extreme of being rash. Right after he finished the pilot, he returned to his job at the park. Even after the series was sold, he still kept working. It was only two days before filming for the show was to begin that

Lee finally called it quits at the park. Even then, he didn't leave completely. He asked to remain on the inactive employee list at the Department of Parks and Recreation, just in case. He was playing it safe.

For two years afterward, as Lee gained popularity on ''The Big Valley,'' his name remained on the inactive list. When he felt secure in his profession, he had his name removed.

Landing the part of Heath Barkley on ''The Big Valley'' was the proverbial big break that every actor longs for. Some actors wait years for that to happen, and unfortunately there are a few who never get it. But for Lee Majors, that athletic youth from Kentucky, it happened with his very first role. He was scared and he was nervous, but he also believed in himself. Just as he had when the doctors told him he might never walk again, Lee knew in his heart that if he tried hard enough and was self-confident enough, he would win.

3

Farrah Fawcett was destined to become a star. After all, she was born with a hauntingly beautiful face and christened with a name that sounded so right for a movie marquee. Farrah is the fetching Charlie's angel's real name. It may sound like it was made up by a press agent, but actually it's the inspiration of Farrah's mother. But agents and interviewers alike are always surprised that Farrah Fawcett-Majors' real name is not something along the lines of Agnes Gooch.

"It is my name," Farrah asserts. "My mother came up with Farrah just so it would go nicely with Fawcett. It has no historical significance. She just made it up."

Farrah was born in Corpus Christi, Texas, on February 2, 1948. That makes her an Aquarius, which may explain why she is so easy-going with such a sunny personality. But Farrah also had other advantages besides astrological benefits. Although not exactly in the lap of luxury, her family was fairly wealthy, and she had many natural advantages. Her father, James, prospered as a pipeline contractor for the oil fields. Her mother Polly never had to work and was content to remain a housewife, looking after her handsome husband and her two girls. Farrah has an older sister Diane, and the family of four was always a warm and close one.

Many of Farrah's old-fashioned and traditional beliefs can be attributed to her upbringing, especially the influence of her mother. Her parents were loving, but held conservative values, and Farrah reflects this today.

"My mother's home is her office," she says, in defense of women who don't work. "She was always content to stay at home. Some people put her down for that. I don't. Lots of women are happy living and working that way."

Farrah's good looks may in part be attributed to her exotic heritage. She has both French and American Indian stock in her background. Despite the fact that Farrah had the beauty and the star-quality name to become an actress, it wasn't a childhood dream. She didn't grow up, like so many other performers, nursing the fantasy of a show business career and thoughts of her name in neon lights.

"One odd thing about me," she confesses. "I never thought about what I was going to be. I've asked my mother what I said on the subject when I was a child, and she said that when I was four or five, I wanted to be a nun. And that's the last time I ever said anything about it.

"I never felt I needed to be a star," says Farrah simply. Surprising words from a girl who could make most men forget all about the likes of Marilyn Monroe and Grace Kelly.

But then conceit has never been Farrah's strong point. People who meet her, expecting to find a stuck-up, self-involved woman, are surprised to find that she's so unassuming.

But then Farrah was never encouraged to feel arrogant about herself as a child. Despite her comfortable home situation, despite her material wealth, despite her great beauty, she was expected to tow the line and behave.

"I was never rebellious as a child," recalls Farrah. "I listened to my parents, helped my mother with the dishes, and studied hard in school."

Another aspect of Farrah's youth that contributed to her traditional outlook was her strict religious upbringing.

Farrah went to W. B. Ray High School in Corpus Christi, where she became very interested in art. She thought about becoming an professional artist, possibly a sculptress. Although her good looks earned her some work in local commercials and a few modeling jobs, show business never entered her mind.

High school was not always a carefree time for the teen-aged beauty. Farrah would be the first one to admit that being so gorgeous as an adolescent was a handicap. While people were dazzled by her beauty, they were also put off and intimidated by it. And the fact that Farrah consistently made good grades, usually straight A's, didn't help matters any. Many times she felt she was resented and even discriminated against because of her looks.

"I remember school being very difficult," she confesses, her ever-present smile turning into a somber look. "Teachers thought I was vain and they were defensive toward me—both the men and the women. Many of them thought I believed all

I had to do was just sit and look pretty to make good grades. . . . In the long run, I didn't get the grades I deserved because of their attitudes.''

It wasn't even so much of a help to be so beautiful as far as social life in high school was concerned. She dated a lot less than her girl friends, who weren't nearly as pretty as Farrah. Just as the girls were easily threatened by her looks, boys felt that a girl who looked like that would be a snob—or that she would turn anyone but a movie star down.

Many times Farrah felt she was being prejudged, many times she felt that she was treated unfairly, but she just kept smiling. Farrah learned that being a beauty can be just as difficult as being ugly, but her family always provided a close base for her, a place where she always felt loved and appreciated.

''I was always protected by my family,'' she admits. ''I liked being protected. It kept me from getting too wise too soon.''

After Farrah graduated from high school she switched bases to attend college at the University of Texas at Austin. She was just eighteen, and it was the first time she had ever been away from home.

One of her elective courses during her freshman year was one in art. Her work for that class was so well received, and she got so much pleasure out of doing the projects, that she decided to major in art. When she had first arrived at college, she had signed up to become a microbiology major. But Farrah dropped those plans in favor of art. Every time she finished a painting or a piece of sculpture, her friends and classmates would want to buy it. They heaped praise upon her efforts, and soon Farrah was shaping her career toward becoming an artist. She became especially interested in both abstract painting and realistic sculpture.

Farrah's beauty at the University of Texas, a school long known for the legions of lovelies who have graced its campus, did not go unnoticed either. She was the first freshman to be named to a select group of girls known as the ''Ten Most Beautiful Coeds.'' Along with citations, the school sent pictures of all the winners out to Hollywood.

Even the agents in Hollywood, as surrounded as they are by some of the most beautiful women in the world, were impressed with the fetching Farrah's looks. Just as in a movie script, a publicist called Farrah up and invited her out to Hollywood. He assured her that she could become famous and rich by working in commercials.

''He said I could make a lot of money doing commercials,'' recalls Farrah. ''I told him no, because at that time, I was having too much fun. You know. There were boys and the parties. I loved college. And at that time, I really wanted to become an artist. I still see my art teacher, professor Charles Lumlauf, whenever I go home.''

So Farrah refused, passing up the chance to go to Hollywood, to stay in college with her active social life and her beloved art courses. She wasn't interested in having a show business career or being famous. Farrah was interested in just being Farrah and having a good time.

Farrah was a typical coed in college. She was a popular sorority girl, who dated some of the handsomest fraternity boys. And she dressed just like a model out of the college issues of fashion magazines. No matter how many exams or how little sleep she had, she always looked great.

"My best friend and I believed in dressing well and looking our best on campus. That was at the time, however, when a lot of art students showed up in class looking like slobs.

"Soon we were nicknamed the 'Jet-Set Twins' because we looked flashier than the rest of the kids and we wouldn't wear cut-off jeans or old clothes to school. We didn't look like hippies—and that disturbed our fellow students. People had trouble dealing with us. It was a strange feeling—to be criticized for looking neat and pretty."

Then too, there were the times that Farrah would come into a party, and all the girls, after one glimpse at this blond beauty, would grasp the arms of their dates for dear life. People always assumed that Farrah was a man-stealer, and they were always wrong about that. She was never interested in going after other girls' dates. She's never been that kind of girl. As a matter of fact, she always has described herself as a "one-man woman," and most of the time in college she dated just one guy.

While some of the girls at the University of Texas agonized over whether Farrah would snatch away their boyfriends, the agents in Hollywood agonized over whether this lovely Southern beauty would make up her mind to come out to Hollywood. They refused to take "No" for an answer. Week after week, they assailed her with phone calls and letters, begging her to come out to Hollywood to make a career in films. All kinds of extravagant offers were tendered her way.

But Farrah wasn't playing hard to get. She wasn't being cool. She just wasn't interested.

"It became a big joke at college," Farrah laughs. "My roommate would say: 'It's Hollywood calling again.' I had never thought about a career as an actress. I wasn't even in a drama class."

Besides, Farrah's father wanted her to stay in school and get her degree. "I want you to graduate," he would lecture her. "I want you to study and get straight A's." For a while, Farrah was content to do that. But then things changed after her junior year and the prospect of returning to school in the fall again did not excite her. She decided it was time, after all, to give Hollywood a whirl.

"Everyone at school was leaving," she explains. "My boyfriend was going to Europe, my girlfriends to different parts of the country, so I thought, why not take the summer and go out there and do commercials."

Once having made up her mind to do just that—and convincing her father—Farrah made the journey out west, chauffeured out to Lotusland by her worrisome parents. They didn't want their younger daughter unleashed in Hollywood without any supervision. To be on the safe side—Hollywood was pretty much Sin City as far as these nice old Texas folks were concerned—they deposited Farrah in an all-girls boarding house.

Farrah immediately got in touch with the publicist who had been urging her all this time to come to California. His name was David Mirisch, part of the fabulous Mirisch family responsible for so many great movies. He had seen Farrah's picture in a newspaper article about the "Ten Most Beautiful

Coeds" and had been instrumental in convincing Mr. and Mrs. Fawcett to allow their daughter to try her luck in Hollywood. Mirisch was influential in building up Farrah's career those first few years.

Farrah did not have to wait long to be noticed by the studios. She didn't have to languish around for years until her big break came. Oh, there were a few rough spots for her after she set up camp at the Hollywood Studio Club (now out of business). But only two weeks of them. After about fifteen days of "crying and hating Hollywood," Farrah waltzed into Screen Gems with her agent and landed a contract for a hefty $350 a week. Along with the contract came offers of acting lessons, horseback lessons, all kinds of lessons to help make Farrah a star. The one course she did sign up for almost immediately was a course in diction, to help her get rid of that thick Southern drawl.

So the tears dried, and Farrah decided to stay awhile. But she was pretty much the babe in the woods as far as Hollywood was concerned. Most of her girlfriends simply wanted to get married, and she was not prepared for the things involved with working and getting a paycheck. When she would receive W-2 forms in the mail, she would tear them up. She didn't know she was supposed to take care of them. Finally, her father asked her about her taxes, and Farrah then realized that she had to do something about those W-2 forms.

While her father was worrying about Farrah's taking care of the business end, her mother urged her to take care of the social part of her life. "Have a good time!" she would say to Farrah, each time they would speak.

But there were some rude awakenings to be found in Hollywood for this sheltered, very protected girl from Texas. Like discovering how much people could use you. Like discovering that there was a different side to life that was not talked about much in Corpus Christi.

But first there was her career to take care of. And one thing that made it easier for Farrah—being in Hollywood, climbing the ladder of success—was meeting Lee Majors. The two of them met about two weeks after Farrah arrived. It was then that things really started looking up for her. Because if they hadn't, Farrah says today, ''I would have turned right around and gone home.''

_____ *4*

"**W**hen I first heard from Lee Majors, I thought he was the rudest man I'd ever encountered."

That certainly doesn't sound like the words of a woman in love. But the speaker is actually Farrah Fawcett, who's been blissfully married to Lee Majors for over four years. Yet their very first meeting certainly was no candlelight and wine rendezvous. They did not fall in love across a crowded room full of strangers and dash madly into each other's arms. If it hadn't been for a little perseverance on Lee's part and a little understanding on Farrah's part, their first meeting might well have been their last. It certainly did not bode well for a future romance.

It all happened shortly after Farrah arrived in Hollywood, fresh from college life at the University of Texas. She had a few glossies, 8″ by 10″, of that gorgeous face, and a perky optimism for her future in the land that made stars. She wasn't quite sure what she wanted to do, perhaps a little modeling and maybe even some acting. In hopes of getting work, she had her agent send around her picture. It not only led to work, but also to romance.

One of the people who spied Farrah's fetching photograph, and was of course suitably impressed with her beauty, was a man named Dave Gershenson. He worked as the publicity agent for Lee Majors. Dave knew that his client, who was then working on "The Big Valley" series, would love to meet this beautiful Texas honey. He snatched up Farrah's picture and rushed over to the studio to show it to Lee.

Always a man of few words, Lee was bowled over and struck speechless when he saw the photograph. Wide-eyed and awed, he kept staring at this newcomer's lovely face and exclaimed, "God! She's magnificent! I'd really love to meet her!" Gershenson managed to finagle her number from a friend so that Lee could call her on the telephone to ask her out.

Excited at the prospect of meeting this beautiful girl, who was moreover a fellow Southerner like himself, Lee's good judgment was temporarily blotted out by his heady infatuation. That same day, he left a curt message at the all-girls boarding house where Farrah was staying. The message was simple and brusque: "Please tell her that Lee Majors will be by at eight o'clock to pick her up."

When Farrah returned from her day of interviews and calls, she got the message and became very angry. She was used to the Texas-college-boy method of courting and chivalry, and she was highly annoyed by this brash and rude young man. Stalking her room like a caged lioness ready to attack, her magnificent blond tresses flying out in all directions, Farrah was fuming. All kinds of furious thoughts filled her pretty head. Who was this guy, anyway? Farrah had heard of Lee Majors, the actor on "The Big Valley" television series, but she had never been introduced to him personally. Who did he think he was, anyway, leaving a message like that for her? She resolved that she would never go out with this rude and arrogant actor. If he called or showed up at her doorstep, she would quickly tell him "NO!"

But then Lee called, full of apologies and Kentucky sweet-talk, and all of Farrah's fierce anger melted away. With a boyish, almost shy sort of charm, Lee asked her to please excuse his brief message. He had been working on location for the series, he explained, and it was hard to get to a phone.

"I'm so sorry to have left that message," Lee said softly. "You know when you work on the set, you can't always get back to a phone, and I just didn't want you to make plans," he said, almost contritely. It was obvious that more than anything else in the world, this handsome actor wanted a date with Farrah Fawcett, new girl in town. He could have probably had his pick of any pretty starlet in town. Instead he was asking her out. That terse message wasn't an insult after all, Farrah realized. It was simply an indication, however rude the manner was and the words sounded, of how much Lee wanted to take her to dinner.

"Yes," said Farrah sweetly and simply, that speech of angry, tell-him-off words quickly evaporating.

33

As arranged, Lee picked Farrah up at her boarding house later that night. When she came downstairs to greet him, her heart started pounding. "It was love at first sight, I guess," she recalls about her first date with Lee.

But despite Lee's obvious infatuation with Farrah, and her instant affection for him, the evening did not go smoothly. It was like a couple of thirteen-year-olds out on a first date, as clumsy and ill-at-ease as they could be. Here were two fabulous-looking people out together, who by all rights should have been having a marvelous, fun-filled evening. But the two of them didn't know what to say to each other. Neither said a word for almost a quarter of an hour. Lee just sat quietly behind the wheel, driving away, and Farrah simply smiled that dazzling grin of hers. There was no small talk, no opening gambits of conversation. Finally Lee did say something, but Farrah couldn't hear him, so she just continued smiling. It turned out later that Lee, bowled over at Farrah's looks, which were even more devastating in person than in the photograph, had complimented her great beauty. But the comment was for naught, since Farrah couldn't hear what he was saying.

"I drove for ten minutes before either of us said a word," Lee reminisces. "I finally said, 'You're really very beautiful.' She didn't hear me. I was mumbling and she had to ask me to repeat it."

After what must have seemed like light years, an eternity filled with long awkward pauses and only a few words of conversation, Lee and Farrah arrived at the restaurant where they were to eat. Farrah asked the waiter for a strange drink combination. Perhaps the sight of the unusual mixture was enough to give her queasy feelings, because after the drink came, Farrah excused herself and vanished for the ladies' room. She remained there, feeling ill, for about half an hour. Finally she came back to the table to rejoin her date.

By this time Lee was worried but he was also upset. He wasn't sure whether Farrah was really sick or whether it was just a case of bad vibes between the two of them. He thought that perhaps she simply did not like him and was trying to get out of the date. Even after she returned to the table, Lee was not convinced that he and Farrah were ever going to hit it off.

But despite the awkwardness of that beginning, Lee didn't want this beautiful girl to escape his grasp. The next day, as both a symbol of their unlikely and unlucky first date, and a symbol of hope for better things to come, Lee sent Farrah a baker's dozen—thirteen—yellow roses. They were the state flower of Texas, and Farrah was touched by his thoughtfulness. From that day on, they've been inseparable.

Lee and Farrah had been dating for several years when they decided to become more serious and date each other exclusively.

In their case, things did work out. Farrah and Lee took the final plunge and became man and wife on July 28, 1973, the fifth anniversary of their first, not-so-promising date. It was a quiet, garden wedding in the bright California sunshine. Just family and a few close friends were invited, and no press was there. Farrah became Mrs. Lee Majors, and added a hyphen and Lee's name to her own, becoming Farrah Fawcett-Majors.

It wasn't Lee's first marriage. He had been wed once before, while still a teenager of seventeen, to his high school

sweetheart, a pretty girl named Kathy. That union had pro-
duced a son, Lee Jr., who is now fourteen. The marriage
broke up in 1965, and Lee Jr. and the first Mrs. Majors live in
Kentucky. Lee's son always visits him during the summer
and he and Farrah get along fine.

The relationship between Farrah and Lee is not one
fashioned according to the dictates of women's lib. Farrah is
more the type of wife who subscribes to the Total Woman
philosophy of pleasing your man and thus pleasing yourself.
She's dependent on Lee and wants him to be the boss in their
marriage. And she speaks proudly and straightforwardly
about those beliefs to anyone who asks about them. She
defines the way they live and love together as an equal
relationship, but one in which Lee has a little bit more
equality.

"I definitely like for Lee to be the strong dominant figure
in my life," she states. "I like for him to say 'I don't want
you to do that because it's not good for you.' Up to a point, of
course. Then there comes the time where I'll say I'm going to
do it, because I want to and that's all.

"I just think," Farrah says serenely, obviously very certain of how she feels and unruffled by what others may think,
"at least for me, that that kind of relationship makes for a
better world."

Surely it makes life in the cutthroat world of Hollywood a
lot easier and a lot nicer for Farrah. She acknowledges that
knowing Lee, having him to lean on during her first year out
in California, made things so much more pleasant for the
fledgling show business star. Of course, she admits, she
could have survived on her own; but there were some tough

times for her, and having Lee by her side made them more bearable.

Friends say that their relationship has made for a more contented and happier Farrah. With Lee helping her make major decisions and solve problems with her career, she is relieved of a large part of the burden. It's startling to find a star of Farrah's caliber as nice and sweet as she is. Those who know her well say her popularity hasn't changed a hair on her golden head, and attribute her gay, easygoing nature to her warm and loving marriage.

For his part, Lee is all hymns of praise and odes of glory to his beloved wife of four years. He dated just about every eligible girl in Hollywood, he says, and he couldn't find one that matched up to Farrah. Not only in beauty, but also in character.

"She's so gorgeous," Lee rhapsodizes. "She's like a little girl. So cute, so beautiful inside.

"And she hasn't changed a bit in the seven years I've known her," he exults happily, describing their fantastic relationship.

In response to women's libbers who would criticize her arrangement with Lee, Farrah asserts that she enjoys doing things for her bionic mate.

"For instance," she says thoughtfully, "I get a kick out of making him cookies. Of course, if he said to me, 'Farrah get in there and make me cookies,' I'd tell him to get in there and make them himself. But we've found out what works for us."

Another thing that works for Farrah and Lee is having her home every night so that they can eat dinner together. Lee arranged for Farrah to have a special rule in her contract which allows her to finish shooting so that she can be home by 7 P.M. But, as she would like to make perfectly clear once and for all, that's not because she must be home to fix his dinner. Usually a housekeeper prepares the meals. But if Farrah wants to cook, she does. "I don't do it because I have to," she declares. "I do it because I love Lee and I love cooking."

Farrah bristles at the descriptions of her dashing home from a frantic day on the "Charlie's Angels" set to fix dinner like some slave. It simply isn't like that.

Sure, sometimes she comes home to cook. But that's because she enjoys doing it and she cares about what she eats.

"My housekeeper doesn't like to cook, and I'm crazy about it," Farrah explains. "What I'd like to prepare would be French dishes with all the sauces, and terrific desserts. But Lee munches doughnuts during most of the day and isn't that hungry when he comes home. So I settle for making things like chicken and a salad."

But that love for the domestic life didn't extend to cleaning up after dinner. Although Farrah is well known in Hollywood for being an immaculate housekeeper, one who gets as much pleasure from a dust-free living room as a good performance in a commercial, she didn't like washing the dishes after their intimate dinners together.

Lee and Farrah like to keep the romance alive, like to keep the sparks flying in their relationship. Each of them drives around during their hectic days in matching Mercedes, which have phones installed in them. They whisper sweet nothings to each other all day long over the phone.

"Sometimes it's the only way we ever get to talk to each other," Farrah claims.

And while Farrah makes Lee some chocolate chip cookies, he's also doing thoughtful little things for her.

"On average," she confesses, "Lee buys me roses every two weeks, and he's always surprising me with little gifts. Like a gold chain with 'I Love You' on it."

As in every marriage, there are times of squabbling and fighting between the six million dollar man and his lovely wife. Times when the hugs and the kisses turn into growls and snarls. Most of the time they get along like two Southern peas in a pod, but there are those occasions when they're at loggerheads.

As Farrah confesses, "Living with the six million dollar man is not that easy a task. He's arrogant and difficult. . . . We fight a lot but not for very long."

Lee is equally candid about bickering with his spouse. While gazing adoringly at the magnificent-looking girl he married, he admits, "There are times I'd like to slug her. But to look at her face is to love her. And who could punch the woman he loves?

"We fight as hard as we love," he reveals, "and love as hard as we fight."

Yet, in spite of the fighting, the state of affairs in the Fawcett-Majors household is pretty much a model one.

"We have a great relationship," exults Lee. "She's just a little ray of sunshine in my life. Aside from being married to her, I'm very proud of what she's done on her own."

Like her modeling career, which thrust Farrah's fetching face on the covers of the top fashion magazines in the country. Or like her acting career, in which she's been propelled into the limelight with her role on the season's hottest show, "Charlie's Angels." Even the fact that she makes more money than Lee does—reportedly over $500,000 a year—doesn't bother him. It makes him all the more proud of his dazzling wife. As a matter of fact, Lee would be the first one to crow about all the money Farrah receives and her tremendous success. Even if Farrah should surpass Lee in the superstardom department, that wouldn't ruffle his male ego.

"Hey, listen," he boasts excitedly. "I hope Farrah becomes the biggest star in the world. That way, if something happens to my career, I won't have to worry. Let's face it, lots of guys are supported by girls. But who could ever say that they were being supported by a girl more beautiful than my wife? The way I figure it, there's no way I can lose in this competition. If something happens to my career, I'll just devote all my time to being Mr. Farrah Fawcett! That's not really what I expect—but it's also not so bad either!"

One thing that *is* bad is how little time Farrah and Lee have together, since they're both working in prime-time series that have weekly episodes. When Lee was doing "The Six Million Dollar Man" and Farrah was just doing modeling assignments, she would often drop by his studio for a surprise visit. Now, because of her own frantic schedule, she has to rise before Lee in the morning and sometimes arrives home later than he does. But Farrah, ever the optimistic soul and positive thinker, takes it all with a grain of salt. The price of success and fame doesn't get her down.

"Things could be worse," she shrugs. "I could be home running the house and never see Lee anyway.

"If I were married to a doctor, I wouldn't see him any more than I see Lee. And in my opinion, being in the same profession has been good in our relationship. Whenever I come home with a problem, Lee's better equipped to understand it."

But it's mostly catch as catch can for those rare moments of togetherness. It is difficult for Farrah and Lee to synchronize their schedules, so they grab every opportunity they can to enjoy each other's company. Even if it means meeting between laundry cycles or hugging between five and six in the morning. When they return home from their busy days on the set, they usually relax by curling up with one another, usually by the fireplace over dinner. That is the time they like the best. They feel so relaxed that their Southern accents, which are held in check when they're emoting before the TV cameras, come out in full drawl. Farrah will speak in those honey-sweet Texas tones, and Lee will answer back in that thick-as-molasses country drawl from Kentucky. Between their Southern-style conversations, there is also time for some husband-and-wife displays of tender loving care.

"We just kiss and hug and all that stuff," Farrah smiles. "Maybe I'll tell him a funny thing that happened on the set, or he'll relate an anecdote about 'The Six Million Dollar Man.' But otherwise, we'll forget about work."

When Farrah won the role of Jill Munroe on "Charlie's Angels," Lee was more excited than she was. He went right out and bought her a special congratulatory gift. It was a tape recorder for Farrah to practice her lines with. When she turned it on to test her voice, she heard an endearing message from her thoughtful husband. Lee had recorded, ''I love you, Farrah.''

That is hardly the reaction of a competitive husband. It's obvious that Lee takes pride in and enjoys Farrah's success as much as she does. And the feeling is mutual. She thinks that Lee's series is just about the best thing going, and naturally that his acting is fantastic!

''When you really love somebody, I don't think competition enters in,'' Farrah explains. ''Lee is very happy and very proud about what is happening for me, just like I am for him.''

And yet, despite her phenomenal rise to the top, her rocketlike surge to become one of the most popular stars on television—all in less than a season—Farrah claims she'd give it all up in a minute for Lee. If he had a fabulous offer for work that could only be done in Europe, a project that would take him away from Farrah for a long period of time, she would seriously consider foregoing her own career plans to join him there. By the same token, she insists that if she were offered a picture that would be shot on location far away from Hollywood, she would discuss the assignment very carefully with Lee. Farrah feels that her career just has to take second place to Lee's. She doesn't feel bad about that, because that's the way she wants it to be. After all, in her mind, ''My marriage comes first,'' she declares. If it were a choice between being Charlie's angel and Lee's loving wife, she would choose the latter every time. Being Mrs. Lee Majors is the most important thing in the world to Farrah.

Farrah says that Hollywood would have been a more unpleasant place to be if it hadn't been for Lee. She knows that the town can be as cutthroat as it can be convivial, and the competition and pressures of the business infect the whole atmosphere. But she met Lee almost at the very beginning, and his gentle but firm guiding hand helped her make it as a newcomer to show business. It's been a lot easier for Farrah to have Lee around, not only for advice, but also for the love and affection she needs. Being married to Lee has been a steady base of reality for her, especially in a city where the fantasy life seems more imporatnt than the day-to-day dramas.

Lee has been described by friends as ''intensely jealous'' about his wife. The talk is that he sizzles if another man takes a long look at his wife. Farrah deftly evades the inevitable questions about Lee's jealousy and states that both of them have insecure feelings about each other working in a business with so many glamorous people.

''Lee wasn't crazy about me getting into this business. He had these insecurities about 'Who is she going to work with?' But then, I had the same insecurities about him. So I figured if I had them, he should too.''

But simply the fact that here are two gorgeous stars, married to each other, but working on different shows, spawns all kinds of vicious rumors. The gossip goes almost hand in hand with their rising popularity. More than once Farrah has heard stories about her going out with this man or that man in Hollywood. At first the tales shocked and upset her, but now she's beginning to realize that it's all part of show business.

As Farrah becomes more of a prominent star, there is speculation that she will leave Lee and go out on her own. Each time the couple has any sort of marital spat, it's blown into major warfare that is prophesied to end in the divorce court. Ever since Farrah started on ''Charlie's Angels,'' there has been talk that she and Lee are breaking up.

This kind of idle talk riles their explosive Southern tempers. Both Lee and Farrah get their dander up when they hear things like this. It not only bothers them, but it also upsets Farrah's mother and father, who are in Texas and can't always call their daughter each time a new rumor springs forth.

Lee became so irritated by the gossip at one point that he took an advertisement out in *Variety* to officially refute the rumors. The ad was actually placed to announce that Lee was making his directorial debut with an episode of ''The Six Million Dollar Man.'' But at the bottom of the page was an important P.S.—''To quiet those rumormongers who are determined to dissolve our marriage in print, let it be known that Farrah Fawcett-Majors and I have never been happier in our seven years together.'' It was Lee's way of dealing with the nasty stories and defending his woman's honor. Very much the old-fashioned mate, Lee rushed to protect his wife's good name.

''Lee can't stand that kind of talk, and it was his way of saying, 'Look, we're okay, leave us alone.' He reacts by becoming sullen and withdrawn and it hurts me to see him sad. That ad was a complete surprise to me, and I was happy to know it meant so much to him to have the gossip squelched that he could take part of that ad to write what he thought,'' says Farrah.

Lee and Farrah are the kind of warm, affectionate couple who believe in showing constant displays of affection to each other. They hold hands in public and wink tenderly at each other across a crowded room at a party. When they're at a social gathering, they often just stand around with their arms entwined about each other, chatting and smiling to other guests. The company they enjoy best in life is each other's. After four years of marriage, they still act like newlyweds.

They take care of each other, and enjoy doing that. Farrah takes care of Lee by making him his favorite kind of cookies, fixing him a drink before dinner, turning on soft music to help her husband relax, just ''taking care of my man,'' she calls it.

And Lee also takes good care of Farrah, by being the protective, secure, and strong kind of person she wants her husband to be. He gives her all his attention and all his love. By helping her pace out the moves in her career and advising her when she needs help with a problem, Lee is very much the strong man in all facets of her life.

''There's one thing I can say about Lee, and that is that he is a gentleman in every respect. He makes me feel very secure. When I'm with him in a crowd, he gives me all his attention. I have never doubted him. It's flattering and very assuring, because, after all, he's a great-looking guy,'' exults Farrah.

Only one thing could possibly add to the connubial bliss

shared by Mr. and Mrs. Majors. That's a baby. But talk of children, which both want very much, has been postponed for a while, since Farrah started her series and her popularity has made her such a big star. But Farrah wants very much to be a mother and can't imagine life without a few little Majorettes around.

"We were thinking of starting a family right away, and then we got notice that my series, 'Charlie's Angels,' was confirmed," Farrah explains. "Lee said, 'Well, there goes another baby.'

"But we'll probably wait a couple of years. . . . It's not that pressing to either one of us, and I want to have time to spend with the child. I believe the first three years are the most important ones in a child's life," Farrah says.

But for now, the important times for Farrah and Lee are the ones they have together. They relish those cozy occasions far more than stardom on TV or the huge, hundreds-of-thousands-of-dollars salary each gets each year. Their marriage may be old-fashioned and out of date as far as some women's libbers are concerned, but it's the kind of marriage that works just fine for Farrah and Lee. One could suspect that their relationship, as they stroll along the Hollywood boulevards arm in arm, is the envy of a lot of their friends. Life in the household of the bionic man and his angel woman is simply great. No wonder Farrah announces gleefully, "I couldn't be happier."

Lee's big break and his first professional role was in "The Big Valley," playing Heath Barkley, opposite Barbara Stanwyck.

Here's Farrah and Lee in their courting days several years ago, before Farrah adopted the layered hairstyle she's famous for today.

Farrah and Lee were married on July 28, 1973, with their proud parents looking on. From left are Mr. and Mrs. Fawcett, Farrah and Lee, and Mr. and Mrs. Yeary.

Farrah and Lee are hardly the Hollywood party type; their favorite company is each other.

You couldn't find a more affectionate couple than Farrah and Lee, who like nothing better than to kiss and hug when they get home from work.

Lee's son by his first marriage, Lee Jr., was an honored guest when
Farrah and Lee were wed in California in 1973.

Farrah played a beautiful, pleasure-loving young maiden of the 23rd century in the movie *Logan's Run,* with Michael York and Jenny Agutter.

_____ 5

Forget about the fact that when Lee Majors won the part of Heath Barkley on "The Big Valley," he had never acted professionally before. Forget about the fact that this was the fledgling actor's first job, and he was nervous as could be about that. There were other problems for the husky Kentuckian to overcome. The role of Heath, set as it was on a ranch in California during the turbulent 1870s, required that Lee be proficient in the saddle. And Lee, despite his Southern upbringing, had never been on a horse.

But with the characteristic practicality and perseverance that has marked Lee's rise in Hollywood from park worker to bionic star, Lee set out to become an adept equestrian. Right away, he went out and bought a horse and practiced riding on the animal every day. Luckily, he had a convenient place to shelter it. Lee had rented a small ranch house near the Pacific Ocean and worked there as a caretaker.

Just a beginner at the acting game, Lee worked on ''The Big Valley'' with Barbara Stanwyck, veteran actress of films and TV. Her TV husband had been the entrepreneur rancher Tom Barkley. Barkley had built up an empire with interests in ranching, shipping, mining, orchards, vineyards, and farming before his death. Now his widow ruled his business with an iron hand and the help of her three sons. Richard Long was the oldest son, Jarrod, who acted as the general head of the family. Peter Breck was the headstrong Nick Barkley. Lee was awed at the experience of working with Miss Stanwyck, one of the biggest names in Hollywood. And his costars, Richard Long and Peter Breck, are also distinguished actors. Then there was Linda Evans, who played Audra Barkley, with whom Lee had studied drama at MGM. All had countless hours of acting credits behind them. But Lee, the shy, reserved young hopeful from Kentucky, was just starting out.

Despite his beginner status, great things were expected of him. Even before the series debuted, on September 15, 1965, Miss Stanwyck, who had been favorably impressed with Majors' test for the role, was touting Lee as a newcomer to watch out for, an actor of great promise.

Lee was flattered by the praise but was anxious that he wouldn't measure up to such great hopes once the cameras started to roll and the action began.

''But what if I don't come through,'' he worriedly asked Miss Stanwyck.

Nonplussed by Lee's anxiety, Barbara smiled and said simply, "In that case, you'll get a kick in the slats from me."

But Barbara was never forced to give Lee a kick in the slats, as he more than fulfilled the complimentary predictions ascribed to him. By the time "The Big Valley" had finished its first season, Lee had received at least six offers from different producers for starring roles in motion pictures. But instead of using his time off from the series to make a foray into films, Lee opted for some rest and relaxation. He wanted to be fresh and physically rejuvenated for his role for the second season.

Understanding Lee's natural nervousness and apprehension about his acting, Barbara Stanwyck went out of her way to be as helpful as possible during Lee's stint with "The Big Valley," especially those first few months. "She doesn't like pushy people," Lee commented back then, in admiration. Their relationship was completely untroubled and serene until the day that they disagreed about how a certain scene should be played. "You can't get along with everybody on thirty shows," remarked Lee, indicating the obvious truth that there is bound to be some conflict from time to time—even in the smoothest of working relationships.

Unfortunately, the press blew the incident up all out of proportion, fabricating a bitter feud between Barbara Stanwyck and Lee Majors. The rumors upset both of them, and even today there are still rumblings about deep ill-feeling between the two. That was how Lee learned the bitter truth about the dangers of gossip in Hollywood. That's when he learned that no matter what happens, gossip and rumors are just an unsavory part of show business.

Much was made of the fact that when Lee first joined the show, his salary was less than the amount that Miss Stanwyck was allotted for her wardrobe—a staggering $20,000. It was a fact that Lee himself mentioned from time to time, not out of any jealousy, but simply wonderment at the huge sums of money that were involved with television.

And he would always follow up any reference to the sum with the sobering realization: "I had no acting experience—I wanted to get my break. It beats working at the park."

"Will you please say one thing," Majors said to a recent interviewer when his current "Six Million Dollar Man" series started, hoping to quell the nasty rumors about him and Stanwyck once and for all. "Barbara Stanwyck was the most professional person I ever worked with, and she taught me a lot."

Originally Lee's role on "The Big Valley," set in the San Joaquin Valley in Stockton, California, in 1878, was supposed to be a one-appearance part. Heath was supposed to appear to claim his inheritance and then be killed. But the producers were so impressed with Lee's ability and his interpretation of the part, that they scratched their original idea and decided to make Heath a running role.

"I was supposed to be the rejected son in the pilot film, unacceptable to the family," reveals Lee. "I was supposed to die in the first episode. Somebody decided to keep my character alive and that's how I survived."

As the first episode went, Heath learned the truth about his identity, that he was the son of Tom Barkley and an Indian maiden. He rushes to the Barkley homestead to demand his rights. After passing a number of tests, Heath gains acceptance to the Barkley family circle and is allowed to take the name of Barkley for his own. In subsequent episodes, Heath becomes closer and closer to the tightly knit clan of Barkleys as they fight to keep order on their 30,000-acre ranch in a era of great change and lawlessness in the West.

The part of Heath echoed many of Lee's own feelings about his past. Heath had many heartbreaking memories of a difficult and often painful childhood—similarly Lee had been troubled by the discovery that his parents were dead and that he was an orphan. Like Heath, Lee had been forced to struggle for his identity, to find that space here on earth which was his. Like Heath, Lee was reaching out to define himself and discover who he really was through love and work. The role of Heath was one that Lee could really empathize with, and this empathy highlighted his acting.

"The Big Valley" lasted four seasons, through May, 1969. Although Lee had originally intended to pull out of the show after the second season to concentrate on films, he changed his mind and decided to stay through the run. He felt that having his own series and establishing himself in television were the most important goals for the time being.

"I've learned the basic techniques of acting," Lee revealed after the series went off the air. "I've tried to improve my craft. I have watched the directing closely. It's important to an actor, especially someone new, to pick up all aspects of the business. I go to dubbing sessions, even turn up at some scoring sessions."

When "The Big Valley" faded into oblivion, Lee didn't

have to worry about playing the role of retired cowhand. Immediately after word got around that the husky actor was available, he won another major running role in another Western series. This one was called "The Men from Shiloh," and it starred James Drury and Doug McClure. Stewart Granger had a cameo role as Colonel Alan MacKenzie, the English owner of the Shiloh Ranch in Medicine Bow, Wyoming, around the 1890s.

As a testimony to his vast popularity, Lee was offered the part of hired hand Roy Tate to increase viewership. Actually, "The Men from Shiloh" was more or less a reshuffling of "The Virginian" series, with James Drury again playing the lead role. When Lee was added to the cast, the ratings for "Shiloh" went up considerably. The increase was enough to substantiate feelings about Majors' appeal to viewers, but not enough to save the series from ultimate cancellation, after only one year on TV. "Shiloh" debuted in September, 1970, and the last show aired September, 1971.

But again, with that luck and perseverance that has always been part of Lee's career, he again escaped the unemployment line. He landed a costarring role in yet another series. This time, Lee exchanged his jeans and work shirts and cowboy suits for a suit and tie. And the setting of the wild and woolly West was changed to the inside drama of a courtroom, as Lee played Jess Brandon in "Owen Marshall, Counselor at Law."

Brandon was the earnest and idealistic junior partner of Marshall, as played by Arthur Hill. Marshall was a contemporary attorney practicing in Santa Barbara, California, who fought valiantly for the rights of his clients, with the aid of his hardworking partner Brandon.

Originally the pilot featured Arthur Hill as Owen Marshall, without the Jess Brandon role. But the part of Jess was added after the series was sold, for a number of reasons. First, Lee had been starring on television in prime-time series for almost six years by that time. He had become a familiar and popular face to millions of TV viewers—in short, an attractive drawing card for any show. It was also felt that Lee, who was considered a talent of great promise, should branch out from his Western parts and play a different kind of role. Lee was a valuable property, then as much as now, to the studio, and they wanted to make use of his abilities and develop his potential as an actor.

As one of the major executives at Universal commented then about Lee, "We believe he's very strong star talent. We have always had great confidence in him."

The experience of playing Jess Brandon again tugged at a common denominator in Lee. Jess was depicted as a former professional football player who had decided to give up pro ball and become a lawyer. Lee also enjoyed some of the provocative themes and exciting drama that were found in the cases that Marshall dealt with.

Yet there were drawbacks for Majors in the series. Despite the great confidence in his acting potential expressed by the studio, Lee's role in the show always remained one of the very definite second-banana type. He starred in just a few episodes, leaving the major part of the legal work to Hill. Lee enjoyed the money he was making, and he appreciated the fact that at last he was playing a secondary role, as opposed to a third or fourth starring part. But he felt frustrated because his talents were not being used in "Owen Marshall" as much as he would have liked them to be.

"I think it's foolish of the studio to pay me big money and then not use me," observed Lee about his role.

There were other aspects of "Owen Marshall" that made Lee uncomfortable. Like the clothes. For a man who had been used to acting and knocking around in a studio for over five years in Western duds, it was difficult to get used to the white-shirt-and-suit-and-tie outfit. Outdoors and casual man that he was, Lee always felt slightly awkward in a lawyer's suit.

"One of the things that bothered me about the show is that I'm a country boy from Kentucky and never really learned how to tie a necktie," Lee confesses. "Also, I like action, staying in shape, and all the exercise I ever got on the show was walking from the counsel table to the judge's bench in the courtroom on Sound Stage 27. It was basically Arthur Hill's show. I had so little to do and so much time off that the series made a great golfer out of me."

Still, Lee did not allow his frustration and discontent to affect his moods and his easygoing relationship with his coworkers. Although clearly disheartened by his secondary status, and the idle time he found on his hands, Lee still contributed a great deal to the show. For one thing, his clowning around and kidding helped to make star Arthur Hill relax and feel more at ease. Hill himself admitted that Lee taught him a lot about the pressures and pace of a nighttime show. Then there were the more practical things about which

Lee could give advice to his star, like camera angles and set design. After all, it was Lee's third series and he was an old hand at the ropes of television production.

During Lee's final year as Jess Brandon, the not-so-visible sidekick of Owen Marshall, his fidgety attitude turned to one of excitement and enthusiasm. The reason? In addition to playing lawyer on that show, Lee was at last starring in his own series called "The Six Million Dollar Man." It may well have been a television first for an actor to star in two different shows for the same network. But at last Lee was thankfully busy, so busy that there was no longer time for perfecting his golf game between scenes. Now it was all Lee could do to sprint from his legal duties on "Owen Marshall" to his bionic chores on "The Six Million Dollar Man." But Lee wasn't complaining. After all, he had what he wanted at last. After ten years in Hollywood, eight years spent in three different series, Lee had finally advanced to a starring role in a nighttime show. No wonder he was bounding with bionic joy!

"The Six Million Dollar Man" was first conceived as an "ABC Movie of the Week." The response to the bionic adventures and Lee Majors in the title role was so overwhelming that it became the pilot for a series. "The Six Million Dollar Man" began as part of a rotating segment of "ABC Suspense Movie," aired on Saturday nights. Soon that segment was so popular that "The Six Million Dollar Man" propelled itself into a weekly series, which now rates as one of the ten most popular shows.

Long before his dream of starring in his own show was realized, Lee was seriously considering making the switch into films. He firmly believed, like most performers, that movies were the big leagues as far as acting was concerned. It was during Lee's "Big Valley" days that he prophesied that he would soon leave television and graduate to feature films, never to return to TV. But somehow, Lee's career in feature films never caught fire. He did two movies that were released to theaters—*Will Penny* and *The Liberation of L. B. Jones*. Neither of them were box office blockbusters, and because of that, his movie career never picked up steam.

The film in which Lee made his debut on the big screen was called *Will Penny*, released in 1968. The movie starred Charlton Heston and Joan Hackett and was a Western. Because of his concurrent acting experience on "The Big Valley," Lee was a natural for the part of Blue, a cowboy range rider who had linked up with Heston. The setting was frontier Montana during the late 1800s, a time when civilization was pushing further westward, and the cowboy was becoming outmoded.

The film received generally favorable reviews by critics who were impressed with this new type of Western. Audiences however seemed confused that this was a Western without the customary trappings. There ware no bloody shoot-outs, no heroic maneuvers, no dance hall girls, no stock characters like brave sheriffs and meddlesome drunks from the saloon. *Will Penny* slipped away very quietly, but today, because of its haunting realism, it is considered somewhat of a film classic, one of the best and most realistic Westerns ever made.

"You know," comments Lee, "that's Charlton Heston's

favorite film. It won several awards. It kind of sneaked out. As we say, it kind of started slow—and then faded off.''

Lee, however, disappointed by the dismal audience turnout, was grateful for the opportunity to work with two such fine actors as Heston and Donald Pleasance, who also was featured in *Will Penny*. He also enjoyed working with Joan Hackett, one of the actresses that Lee admires most in show business. It was the first film for Lee, and unlike so many other first efforts that are grade D and junk, *Will Penny* was a film credit that he could really be proud of.

''Chuck Heston admits it's one of the best films he's ever made,'' says Lee, ''and I agree. I think he and Joan Hackett were marvelous.''

Lee's second film was *The Liberation of L. B. Jones*, which was released in 1970. It starred Roscoe Lee Browne in the title role of a black man struggling against racial prejudice in a small Tennessee town.

In perhaps some of the finest acting he has ever done, Lee Majors played an idealistic, hopeful young lawyer from the North, in what was to be a foreshadowing of his ''Owen Marshall'' days a year later. He is Lee J. Cobb's nephew and arrives to work with the senior lawyer. He is outraged with the rampant racial injustice and bad race relations in the town and tries to bring about a change. The role was pretty much of a stock character, the young and uncorrupted idealist who wants to change the world and refuses to compromise. Yet Lee rose above the confines of that stereotype to create a truly memorable character.

The Liberation of L. B. Jones, despite its explosive subject matter, fared not much better than *Will Penny* at the box office. So Lee devoted his full talents and abilities to TV.

But he has expanded his acting repertoire with several roles in made-for-TV films. Lee starred in such fine productions as *The Ballad of Andy Crocker*, *Weekend of Terror*, and recently, the acclaimed *Francis Gary Powers Story*.

Of course, Lee would love to develop his acting gifts with other roles in feature films, especially if the parts and the movies are right. But right now, he's very busy with his bionic chores—unless the perfect project or the opportunity to team up with Farrah should lure him away from his series. Despite the worldwide attention awarded to film stars, Lee has always said, "I'm in show business for fun and profit, not fame."

_____ 6

When Farrah Fawcett first started her career climb out in Hollywood, she had a big problem. She was just too pretty for most roles. Her golden-girl looks were perfect for pushing products like toothpaste and shampoo—consumers could fantasize they just might turn out like that if they used the products. But forget acting roles like housewives, secretaries, teachers, etc. Casting directors thought she was too beautiful to be believable. Normal people just didn't look as good as Farrah did.

So the bulk of Farrah's work came from doing commercials. That kind of work proved to be so lucrative that she temporarily shelved her acting ambitions. It wasn't that she wasn't interested in acting—she just didn't want to be a poor starving actress, sacrificing all for her art. And she didn't really like having to play down her looks.

Farrah started in commercials by flashing those perfect white teeth for an Ultra Brite spot. Soon she was using that gorgeous face and feline body to sell everything from cars to hair shampoo. With that waterfall of golden hair, she posed for a series of Wella Balsam shampoo ads that triggered the craze for the Farrah Fawcett hairdo. People didn't know what her name was back then, but they all wanted to have their hair just like hers.

"I felt I didn't have the drive to be an actress," recalls Farrah, about those beginning days in Hollywood. "I came out to Hollywood assuming it would be just for the summer. Then everything started happening fast. . . . I said to myself: 'This is terrific! I'll go back home when I feel like it!' "

Farrah began to be recognized, as that girl, what's-her-face, from one advertisement or another. Fans who didn't know her name would greet her on the street with "Hey, Ultra Brite!" or "Hey, creamy!"—referring to her appearance in a Noxzema skin cream ad. She became as famous as—well, as famous as the star of a nighttime series, which she is today. Only no one knew her name.

"I guess I have a memorable face," Farrah says, typically understating her appeal.

The money started to roll in, and Farrah quickly became one of the highest-paid models in the business. She made over $100,000 a year, certainly more than many actresses whose names are household words. She became one of the six hottest models and frequently in demand by advertising agencies, along with girls like Susie Blakely, Jaclyn Smith, and others.

While Farrah may be reluctant to toot her own horn about her astounding career as a model, her husband Lee is not.

"You know, Farrah actually made over $30,000 in just one day shooting TV commercials," Lee boasts. "She's been pulling in well over a quarter of a million dollars a year just doing odds and ends in the TV commercial business since back in the days when I couldn't even get a job. Sure, I've got one of those really hot TV series of my own now, but I'm not as wealthy as Farrah is."

As she appeared in commercial after commercial, her lithe body easing through the ads, her dazzling face and figure were causing minor upheavals in homes all over America. "Who is that beautiful girl?" man after man would sigh, their hearts pounding madly as Farrah slipped through her routine.

As an example of her knock-out appeal, there's the story of the commercials she did with Joe Namath, that great football hero, for Noxzema Shaving Cream. The reaction to the ad was not mostly for pigskin giant Joe, but rather for that nameless but angelic-looking creature who lured Namath in the ad. Mail poured into the Noxzema offices by the sackful, with people wanting to know who that beautiful girl was.

Farrah was as choosy about the products and magazines she posed for as she was about the money she was to receive for each assignment. (She's always demanded that she be paid well for what she does. As she explains it, "You work too hard in this business not to be paid well.") When it came to fashion magazines and covers, she only wanted to be associated with the best. If the magazine wasn't right, Farrah would turn down the offer. She felt from the beginning that she could be selective about her career choices and she was right.

"*Town and Country, Vogue, Harper's,* and *Cosmopolitan* are the ones I've chosen," explains Farrah, indicating a list of the best fashion magazines in the country. "I agreed to do *Cosmopolitan*, but I thought the photography made me look hard. The lipstick was too red and I wanted to wear less makeup and to have my hair softer."

Farrah may not have been so pleased with her picture on the cover of *Cosmo*, but it was that cover which really propelled the Farrah craze. Millions of women would march into their neighborhood hairdresser with that cover under their arms and tell the beautician—"I want to look like that!" Even if they were short or brunette or frowsy or plain. Suddenly practically every female wanted to look like Farrah.

To date, Farrah has made over 100 commercials and posed for even more ads. Her beauty has been used to push products like milk, airline travel, soft drinks, sun glasses, makeup.

Farrah feels today that her career might have been shaped differently had she not met Lee right away and then determined to stay in Hollywood with him.

"I probably would have gone to New York more, modeled more," admits the tawny beauty. "But I have no regrets. I'm glad I didn't rush into a film career. I'm better prepared now and without the commercials I've done, I would be unrecognized today. Those commercials provided my training since I never took drama."

Gradually, Farrah began to land some acting roles in

addition to her work in commercials. Her first film was a small part in the Claude LeLouche movie called *Love Is a Funny Thing*. Then came a part in the TV movie *The Feminist and The Fuzz*.

After she finished her first commercial, she was firmly informed by the director that he was taking her out to dinner. And being independent, that sparked Farrah's fiery Southern temper. She refused and the director told her, in no uncertain terms, that he had the power to keep the commercials off the air. Farrah let him have it, blasting him for his insolence. In the end, Farrah didn't go to dinner with the director, and the commercial was never aired. But she doesn't regret a minute of it and would do the same thing tomorrow if it happened again.

Then Farrah was always running into people in show business who dismissed her as a dumb blonde who couldn't act.

''I got so tired of people saying I was 'too pretty' to play a waitress, or telling me, 'No one will believe your husband left you.'

''People are always saying, 'Oh sure, she's pretty, but can she act?' You constantly have to prove yourself. . . . You know, there really aren't that many good roles for great-looking women! There used to be—but no more.''

Farrah's prettiness came to be quite a problem when she played the role of the ingenue in the film *Myra Breckinridge*. Starring in the film were two well-known actresses—Raquel Welch and Mae West. According to various reports, there was enough animosity between Raquel and Mae, without this beautiful blond newcomer coming along and threatening their star egos even more. It wasn't a warm and wonderful working relationship as far as Farrah was concerned.

The film convinced Farrah of one thing. If she wasn't going to enjoy a project, no matter how much she was going to get paid, she wouldn't do it. Having a hard time wasn't worth it. Life was too short for that, she decided.

"The movie convinced me that if I couldn't have fun on a set and had to worry about other people's egos, it wasn't worth it. So from now on, I won't do anything unless I have a good time and am paid extremely well."

That's one of the reasons she's always expected to have a big paycheck when she has to get up early to film a series role. She was used to lying in bed until around eight-thirty or nine, but that stopped when she landed the regular role of Harry's neighbor and sometime love-interest on "Harry O," starring David Janssen. Then she started getting up at five, and Farrah wanted to be paid well for that inconvenience.

Farrah had appeared on a number of series, before the steady "Charlie's Angels" major role. Her TV credits include stints with Lee on two of his shows—"Owen Marshall" and "The Six Million Dollar Man." She would usually do one show a season. Lee and she would go over the scripts to find a part that was just right for her.

"I can have fun with her," exclaims Lee, on the subject of working with his wife. "The first year she did one and before we started, she thought: 'I get to wear beautiful clothes and look pretty and everything.' So we naturally put her in a space suit! She was the first lady astronaut and she spent the whole show walking around in this space suit which was made for a man! And they're very uncomfortable. . . . It's like being in a portable sauna all the time! And we filmed it at Edwards Air Force Base—which is not your most beautiful location.''

Farrah has shone in the made-for-TV movies she's done, like one called *Murder on Flight 502,* and another, *The Great American Beauty Contest,* about a beauty competition, in which she naturally played a contestant and starred with Eleanor Parker. It was that latter film in which Farrah displayed a remarkable flair for comedy, a timing and zest that could make her the modern Carole Lombard—any day she decides she doesn't want to be the contemporary Marilyn Monroe.

Farrah's second film, *Logan's Run,* a futuristic drama that also starred Michael York and Jenny Agutter, was released in 1976.

She played a pleasure-loving young maiden of the twenty-third century, living along with other earthlings in a domed city. They were all survivors of a great catastrophe and were living it up until they reached the age of thirty. At that time, each person had to submit to a ritual on a carousel-type contraption, where they were supposed to experience rebirth. Actually, the machine, run by centrifugal force, exploded the victims bodies as they soared toward the top of the carousel. It was a dismal view of a future society in which only the very young can survive.

Farrah mulled over the ''Charlie's Angels'' role for a while before she decided to accept. She was already making a good star-sized salary from her commercial work, and she didn't know if she wanted to get involved with the hard work and demands of a weekly series.

But Farrah accepted the role of Jill Munroe, and "Charlie's Angels" quickly became one of the most frequently watched shows on the air waves. She was glad she made that decision.

"Let's face it," admits Farrah. "It's nice to have all the money I made from commercials. I was doing very well. But it's also nice to be finally recognized by name, to have fans know who you are, not to be just a face from an ad. You can't really be famous unless people know who you are."

"I know I am limited as an actress and there are things I cannot do, and one of them is play Christie Love with guns blazing. . . . If there's something I want and I can draw somebody in with my femininity and catch them off guard, and get it, well, what's wrong with that?

"What I do best is to be me in front of a camera. I know how to make men laugh, how to make a male respond."

Life is not always a case of bionic bliss for the six million dollar man. At least Lee Majors doesn't find it so. Sure, he's the star of a top-rated series, one of the most popular on television, and makes over $20,000 each week. Sure, he's one of today's most beloved and adored male stars. But despite the cybernetic charges of his character, sometimes it can be tough.

"How do you think it feels when you're breaking down a door, and the prop men forget to pull out the pins?" sighs Lee, grimacing at the memory of the pain of muscle meeting metal. "I've been jarred right up to my teeth, breaking through.

"I'm supposed to be able to bend bars as some sort of superhuman being, but sometimes the bars don't bend. But I'm not really complaining. After sitting around a TV courtroom for three years with "Owen Marshall," I enjoy this. It keeps me in shape," adds Lee, towering over cast and crew, his husky but trim physique illustrating his statement.

The character Lee plays, that of reconstructed Steve Austin, was in pretty bad shape before he reemerged as the six million dollar man. Steve was a former astronaut who had walked the moon. He was critically injured, near death, in a terrible accident that occurred when he was testing a "lifting body" from a B-52 plane. The accident that befalls Steve is so horrible that he is nothing more than human scrap—he's lost both legs, an arm, an eye. But with the help of some advanced technology, plus the skill of aeromedical surgeons, Austin is put back together again. And there are some added bonuses. He is completely scientifically rebuilt and emerges as a combination of machine and human. He has three new mechanical limbs and is about 100 times as powerful as he was before. Austin becomes what is known in the field of science as a Cyborg. He's a superman kind of hero, with incredible speed, strength, and vision. Steve can jump easily from thwarting a hostile foreign power to zeroing in on a snarling lion without batting a bionic eyelash.

The scientists' reconstruction of Steve Austin has left him with such endowments as a pair of bionic legs that can run up to sixty miles an hour, a synthetic arm with superhuman strength, and an electronic eye that can focus on scenes hundreds of yards away. With such extraordinary abilities, Steve can adeptly fend off enemies of the government. He tackles high-risk missions for the agency OSI, which uses his bionic skill to foil subversive powers.

"He can run like a horse and swim like a fish and hit like a piledriver,'' boasts Lee. "But he's no robot. He's vulnerable. He can think. He can hate. He can love.''

The object of the bionic man's affections was none other than a woman with similar man-made electronic capabilities. During an episode of "The Six Million Dollar Man," Steve met his cybernetic match—Jaime Sommers (played by Lindsay Wagner). His all-too-human and unrobot-like heart beat madly for the pretty bionic woman, who had, like him, been the victim of a serious air crash. During that romantic episode, however, the love story ended on a tragic note. Jaime suffered another accident and died during further reconstruction efforts.

But the fans didn't want the bionic woman to die. Angry protest letters arrived at the Universal studios where "The Six Million Dollar Man" is filmed, decrying the untimely death of superwoman Jaime. The result was that she was reborn again in her own series called "The Bionic Woman."

"I thought she died on the operating table," explains Majors. "So did other people. But I find out she wasn't quite dead and she had been revived. I'm mad because they didn't tell me she was alive.

"But she doesn't remember me. I take her to some of the places we visited together before. But she seems to have lost all memory of our former acquaintance.''

The romance of the bionic man and the bionic woman is one reason why Lee gets so much joy out of the role. He pooh-poohs those critics who say his show is just a comic strip come to life. It's more than a combination of Batman and Superman. "The Six Million Dollar Man" may have a few electronic parts, but above all he's a human being.

''There's a fine line of distinction you have to keep in mind with this program. You have to hold the science and the technical stuff down to what's necessary—only make use of it to get the character out of trouble. You mustn't use it to show off. Otherwise, no adult would watch it.''

Cast and crew on the show feel that the popularity stems from the fact that Steve is an old-fashioned, inspiring kind of hero. Harve Bennett, executive producer of ''The Six Million Dollar Man,'' says: ''Call it escapist, but in this era of public scandal and cynicism, I felt the time was right for the old-fashioned idealistic hero—like the Lone Ranger or Gary Cooper—who comes along to fight evil. But our guy couldn't be invincible like Superman. With all his powers, he had to be questioning, vulnerable, and in jeopardy every so often—so that the audience would root for him and empathize with the human part of him.''

How does a basically human guy like Lee Majors accomplish those superhuman feats on the show? The answer is a little trick photography and some ingenious thinking.

For example, how does Lee perform those fantastic leaps from the ground to the tops of tall buildings? Sometimes the bionic jumps are accomplished with the help of a trampoline, that is either hidden behind an object or else in the ground. Other times Lee, or a stunt man who looks like him, will jump down from the building and then the film is reversed.

Graced with an arm of superhuman strength, the bionic man can be found bending bars, ripping apart walls and doors, lifting cars. Again, in stunts like these special effects are used. Doors can be made from balsa wood or another thin, easily breakable material. The doors can also be partially removed from the hinges so they're easier to take off.

How does Lee stop a car? It's easy enough to do when the special effects crew is helping him. He puts his hand on the front bumper. Then the car backs up. The film is reversed so that it looks like the car is speeding ahead and Lee appears to be stopping it with just a mere brush of his hand.

When Lee hoists a heavy car, it looks like he has the strength of Hercules. Actually, the car is lifted by a special effects man offscreen with a high-pressure air hose. When the vehicle is to be turned over, a hydraulic jack is used, in combination with a crane.

And if the bionic man tosses around heavy objects like rocks and tires with nary a strain, it's because the objects are actually balloons camouflaged to look like the heavy objects. Sometimes an air cannon will propel an object into the air to make it look like Lee is hurling it.

Despite the help of technology in achieving his superhuman feats, Lee has emerged through it all with some very human cuts and bruises. When he crashes through a door made out of tin foil to simulate metal, he's often burst through with some nicks and bruises. The same thing can happen when he tears a metal bar.

Yet, despite these physical hardships, Lee is happy that at last he's the star of a series. The physical hardships pale beside his mental satisfaction and pride that he is finally the main man in his own show.

"It has taken me a long time to really become the star of a TV series," he explains. "In 'The Big Valley,' I had the fourth or fifth lead. Then, in the next season, when I appeared in 'The Men from Shiloh,' I became the third lead. In 'Owen Marshall,' I'm the second lead. And now finally, and at last, I'm the star of a series."

The wear and tear on his body that Lee endures in his bionic acrobatics hasn't seemed to lessen his impish sense of humor any. He will often finish a strenuous scene with a wide grin and a witty joke. One day, after vanquishing four evil-doing karate experts, in the midst of a blinding blizzard, Lee felt revved up enough by the exercise to suggest another round.

A large part of the appeal of "The Six Million Dollar Man" is that it's just one step away from reality. It's hardly idle fantasy, but futuristic science fiction. With technology so advanced, it's just possible that scientists could produce a bionic man—one made up of human as well as electronic parts. Semirobots with human feelings and thinking patterns may be just around the corner of the next decade. If a man can land on the moon and send a spaceship to Mars, then scientists will be able to synthesize a human robot out of machine parts.

Actually some of Lee's bionic derring-do is based on fact. The arm that he uses to swat away an army of predators or juggle a gigantic rock is modeled after a prosthetic arm, revolutionary in nature, that was invented at the UCLA Medical Center.

"The arm has plastic skin that looks and feels like real skin," explains Lee. "It's battery operated, and when they hooked it to my shoulder, I could raise and lower it, and even turn the wrist. Later, they expect to be able to connect the arm directly to the nerve ends of an amputee. The impulses from the nerve endings then might be amplified with atomic power and miniature motors to make the arm maybe even better than a real arm.''

Who knows what concepts and inventions ''The Six Million Dollar Man'' might trigger in the halls of scientific laboratories? It just may be that some ingenious worker, inspired by Lee's feats, will come up with the technical know-how to help accomplish that—without the gimmickry of trick photography and special effects. Someday they may be selling bionic eyes as fast as they now sell bionic man dolls.

Steve Austin, the reconstructed astronaut who became the bionic man, has emerged as one of the great heroes of today. He's the charging white knight of the space age. He's the valiant warrior, helping good triumph over bad, with the aid of some fancy technological innovations.

One of the show's producers, Lee Siegel, sums it up this way: ''In an era of the antihero, Steve Austin is unashamedly a genuine romantic hero . . . a hero in the best sense of the word.

''Steve is also a hero youngsters can imitate. . . . It happens our hero does have something the young viewers like to imitate: the bionic action, which is depicted on the series through slow motion and which is suggestive of power and strength.''

The fans become so involved with the bionic feats that Steve accomplishes that they often write to the studio themselves with suggestions of new superman tricks for him to perform. It's another example of how credible the series is, how ''The Six Million Dollar Man'' is science fiction that could be tomorrow's front page news.

One viewer wrote in to say that Steve should squint to trigger the infrared nighttime sight in his bionic eye. Another viewer wrote that Steve should never sweat from his bionic right armpit—electronic parts don't have those kinds of problems.

The kinds of problems that Lee Majors has these days are those which arise from the superman image that goes along with his bionic character. It is difficult for people to separate the man from the small-screen role. Much to Lee's chagrin and often embarrassment, people somehow expect that he's just as capable of the bionic acts in real life. Lee complains that he can't go into bars because all the other customers want to arm wrestle with the six million dollar man. He admits that he has even let his tennis and golf game lapse on the celebrity circuits, because people expect nothing less than Arthur Ashe– and Arnold Palmer–type performances from the bionic man. Yes, there can be trouble when you're the star of a science fiction series with a superhuman hero—but Lee wouldn't trade a minute of it.

Now that Lee has the character of Steve Austin, with all his electronic paraphernalia, down pat, there are other areas of the show he'd like to explore. This past season he was responsible for directing three of the shows, including a football story called ''One of Our Running Backs Is Missing.'' The show featured football giants Larry Csonka and Dick Butkus. Lee jokingly referred to it as the television version of *The Longest Yard,* the gridiron comedy-drama film that starred Burt Reynolds.

Explaining his inclination to do more than act, Lee says, "After you've done a show for a year, you have the character down pretty well. There's nothing there to stir up the juices for you anymore. If you're in TV series as long as I've been and don't know more than just acting, you've been wasting your time. And I've been curious. I've followed the director's work and I know every camera shot."

Although "The Bionic Woman" was spun off, in typical series regeneration fashion, from "The Six Million Dollar Man," don't expect another cybernetic series. There have been dribblings that the next step would be a show called "The Bionic Boy." Such a character was introduced on a special two-part segment of "The Six Million Dollar Man," and featured Vincent Van Patten in the role. But Lee has an agreement with the producers that a spin-off won't happen until his own show is off the air. And, according to the show's popularity, Lee's fans would be broken-hearted if that day ever came.

Wanted: A beautiful blond actress, with a lean athletic body. Must have pearly white teeth and smile a lot. Must have flowing, slightly tousled hair. Above all, must look as much like Farrah Fawcett as possible.

Those are roughly the requirements that the producers of "Charlie's Angels" will be looking for, should Farrah win her contract dispute and leave fellow actresses Jaclyn Smith and Kate Jackson behind to carry out Charlie's sleuthing for him. While rumors abound that she is holding out for the kind of sky-high appearance fee that someone like Peter Falk gets—something in the neighborhood of $100,000 to $150,000 per show—the truth is that Farrah is prepared to cash in on her popularity and head for a movie career. After all, she wasn't that eager to do a series to begin with. The combination of long days when Farrah must get up at four or five in the morning and the conflict of two spouses starring in different TV shows, both competitive in the ratings, has made her think it's better to be an earthly wife than a Charlie's angel.

Meanwhile, with these behind-the-scenes battles being waged over Farrah's right to leave, the action on the scenes of the ''Charlie's Angels'' show makes it one of the hottest new series in a decade. You can forget about Sam Spade and Kojak. And Columbo can just shuffle along in his weather-beaten raincoat. The most popular crime-fighting detectives of today are a group of heavenly beauties named Charlie's angels. The show is a new and feminine twist on the private detective yarn, and some forty million viewers think they're nothing less than a godsend. After all, what could be better than three private investigators who not only uphold law and order, but are also gorgeous? Just one glance at the trio of sleuths—Farrah, Kate Jackson, and Jaclyn Smith—could make a bank robber drop his gun and a would-be murderer forget the name of his intended victim. Criminals lucky enough to be apprehended by Charlie's angels never had it so good.

The basis of the show is this—three young women, intelligent, athletic, and trained in police work, are sent out on special assignments by their boss, a man named Charlie. Charlie is never seen, not even by the angels themselves. His instructions are issued forth to them over an intercom or the telephone. Then the lovely angels wend their way out, to health spa, prison farm, roller derby, fashion house, race-track clubhouse, to catch the culprit or culprits Charlie wants them to nab. Using disguises, fake names, wigs, and phoney accents, the wily angels bring the murderers, thieves, embezzlers, con artists, and just downright rascals in this world to justice. And all of their brave efforts are extended with humor and with ease, as the eye-catching threesome glides almost effortlessly through the most hair-raising situations without losing their cool. Or without messing a curl or losing a false eyelash. Who cares if the angels seem a little less real than your garden variety gumshoe? They're superwomen, and people love them for it. Fantastic and incredible? Sure. But in the end, what the heck?

Each show begins with the background words of the mysterious Charlie—actually the voice of actor John Forsythe. "Once upon a time," he intones, "there were three little girls who went to the police academy . . . but I took them away from all that." The angels are then summoned to duty by Charlie's assistant, John Bosley, who is always visible on screen in the person of actor David Doyle. Bosley holds a summit conference with the angels, who've come in from swimming pool, horseback riding, or sunbathing, and plays them the tape with Charlie's latest instructions on it plus some video background material of the scene of the crime. Then the angels are off—set to do their duty and defend the law.

Each of the trio is as different and distinct on screen as the actresses who play them are in real life. The leader of the angelic pack is Sabrina Duncan, played by former "Rookies" star Kate Jackson. Sabrina's logical and pragmatic mind always zeros in on the problems the threesome must face. She's the intellectual of the group, with a fluency in five languages, and a knack for spouting out cold, hard facts. She's also fearless and can attack the most dangerous situation with nary a shiver of her lanky body. When trouble strikes, Sabrina keeps her cool.

Jill Munroe, the girl Farrah plays, makes up for her lack of intellectual astuteness with athletic prowess and a zany sense of humor. She's a sport enthusiast and can perform just about any sport as well or better than a man. Jill can throw a karate chop or shoot a gun with the best of them—male or female. Her ever-ready sense of humor springs up in the most spine-tingling situations. Her life may be on the line, but Jill can still crack a joke.

Kelly Garrett, played by Jaclyn Smith, knows the ropes of just about any circumstance that comes up. In her checkerboard career, she's held jobs as a Las Vegas showgirl, an airline stewardess, and a cocktail waitress. When there's a nefarious criminal to be dealt with, Kelly puts aside her natural politeness and points her gun at her man with a steely charm. Calm and sweet, she's a good buffer between the iron-nerved Sabrina and the gaminesque Jill.

The three girls are different in background and personality, but as a trio of private investigators determined to squelch crime, they get alone fine. They have a unique sort of friendship. Each girl contributes something special to the unit and they help each other out in ticklish situations. They don't compete, they're not rivals, they just work hard together to do their jobs. Then it's off to pursue their very separate lives, packing in their pistols for the day. They don't fight over men or tear each other's hair out over a dress. They're all good pals, using the buddy system to complete their chilling assignments for Charlie.

The show was inspired by "Police Woman." Executives decided that if the sleuthing of pretty Angie Dickinson was so popular, then a trio of comely detectives who were nothing less than spectacular-looking would be even more popular. They were right. "Charlie's Angels" clobbered its competition and rose to the top of the Nielsen ratings when it was still a newcomer to the TV scene.

It's unusual that three such stunning beauties captivate women as well as men. It used to be that a knock-out star on a television series could have the men swooning in their armchairs, but the women would turn green with envy and turn off the sets. But "Charlie's Angels" are not just pretty faces. They're tough and free-spirited and independent. They have rough jobs to do, and they do them well. They may take their orders from a man, but they go out on their own and improvise their own solutions to the problems they face. There's no situation they won't tackle or handle. The more dangerous their tasks, the more female viewers like it. "Charlie's Angels" have forsaken the dish rag and the kitchen sink and the secretarial pool to pursue action and adventure, but they haven't forgotten their sense of fashion and beauty. They're well dressed and chic, even in the most hair-raising climaxes, and always have their makeup in place.

It may not be the true-to-life detective story, but then executive producer Aaron Spelling says, "Anyone who thinks these girls are private detectives is nuts . . . On this show we're more concerned with hairdos and gowns than the twists and turns of the plots."

The clothes that the angels wear are indeed stunning. They

always look as glossy and put-together as if they'd stepped out from the pages of a fashion magazine. Even when they're dressed in jeans, they wear French jeans, specially tailored and fit, that run around seventy dollars a pair.

And their hairdos must always be perfect. The show's hairstylist, Naomi Cavin, confirms this. ''Farrah and Jaclyn have made fortunes on their hair and they know exactly how it should be. And Mr. Spelling doesn't want them to appear on the set until their hair is right, no matter how long it takes.''

As irrelevant as hairdo and dress may be to the machinations of clever and effective detective work, it makes ''Charlie's Angels'' a big hit. Particularly in England, with the royal family. The producer's office of the show received an official request from Buckingham Palace in London for an autographed picture of the angels. Apparently they're a big favorite with Prince Philip, husband of Queen Elizabeth. Immediately a beautiful 11'' x 14'' color portrait of the trio was dispatched with the inscription: ''To her Royal Highness, Queen Elizabeth II, and Prince Philip, Duke of Edinburgh—Congratulations on your Silver Jubilee.''

''I can't really put my finger on why the show is such a big hit,'' says Farrah Fawcett, although many people feel her feathery-haired appearance on the series is in large part responsible. ''I think people want to see some glamour, some clothes, some hairstyles, you know—they want to see girls.''

And there's a special feeling, a camaraderie, between the girls that comes through for the fans. It's like a magic bond that ties each of them together.

''The series wouldn't work as well if it was three different people doing it," declares Kate Jackson. "We have a strange chemistry between us. It's like a sorority."

The special relationship is apparent even between scenes, when the angels are just kidding around with each other. Yes, they really do get along, in spite of the tense schedules and the fact that all three have to rouse themselves at the crack of dawn to be made up and coiffed for the day's escapades.

"There's a lack of ego on the series," declares Farrah. "It's no fun to run up against any unpleasantness, but on 'Charlie's Angels,' I get along great with the other actresses."

Jaclyn Smith, another member of this mutual admiration society, proves that there doesn't have to be bitter competition among three gorgeous actresses, when she says, "Farrah's very athletic and the show makes wonderful use of her skill in sports. Kate's the best driver on the show, but it's scary to be in a car with her. She keeps her foot on the gas all the time."

And Kate Jackson also echoes the great working relationship of the trio. "I know people expected there should be a rivalry on this show, but we get along terrifically. I think it's kind of sad that people expect that we three would be at each other's throats all the time. We girls are lucky in the sense that we all have a good sense of humor."

The angels' days are full of actress chores, such as checking wardrobe and having their hair and faces taken care of so that they always look heavenly. On the set they are trailed by hairdressers and makeup men everywhere, to smooth a stray hair and to touch up a faded lipgloss. Male stars don't have the hassles the angels do with their coiffure demands and wardrobe changes. But when you must look glamorous in every scene, you have to work hard to be that way.

And there are definite compensations for toiling away so diligently on "Charlie's Angels." During shooting breaks, each of the trio can relax and put her feet up in the plush comfort of her own Pace Arrow mobile home, which costs in the neighborhood of $25,000. The homes are stocked with fresh flowers and fruit and other amenities daily. If a gown or a bikini that they wear in costume strikes one of the threesome's fancy, she may keep it for her own use. The show allows them to have any clothing they've worn on the series for their own use. They're certainly pampered creatures, with a whole retinue of crew hired just to make sure their needs are satisfied. With all the extras and the luxuries, it's no wonder that the budget for each episode costs roughly about $345,000, which is probably the biggest series budget in history. After all, beautiful girls must be well taken care of.

And the three actresses take care of each other too. They support each other in their work. They stick up for each other and offer comfort to a crestfallen angel, if she's tired or in a bad mood. If one of them is late or muffs a line, the others make excuses for her. They understand and empathize with each other's feelings. "If I see Kate and she's sad," explains Farrah, "I'm sad too."

Recently, on Kate's birthday, all the angels planned for a big celebration. Jackie had a cake made and decorated with three figurines on top. The dolls were models of the angels—one was a blonde and the other two were brunettes.

Occasionally there are tense moments because of the fierce

pressure, but nothing more serious than a case of frazzled nerves or a temper flare-up because of fatigue. Despite the stories, there are no feuds over who has the best lines to say, who has the best outfits, who gets the most attention. Quips Farrah, with her characteristic lighthearted humor, "The only time we have any conflict is when we knock each other down racing for the doughnut wagon."

Well, there was one sticky occasion. Jackie arranged for her large standard poodle named Albert to have a recurring role in "Charlie's Angels." Soon, Farrah was suggesting how her black Afghan named Satchel could also have a running part in the series. It was well known that Kate Jackson had a dog, a husky named Catcher, that she might similarly want slated for stardom. Finally, the plans for Albert to make his acting debut were dropped. It was probably just coincidence, but it may also have been a case of squelching a problem before it got serious.

Most of the problems are those resulting from the physical hazards of doing a nighttime weekly series with lots of action. During the filming of a chase sequence, Farrah was injured by a fast-moving race car and hurt her leg so badly she had to go to the hospital. She's lost about ten pounds from the rigors of the shooting during twelve-hour days, sometimes seven days a week. Jackie had a rude shock when Farrah threw her over her shoulder in a judo-type maneuver. Jackie hit the ground so hard that she bounced. Both Kate and Jackie, who are single, complain about how the series has cramped their social life. They're so dog-tired at the end of the day that there's nothing left to do but go home, eat, and fall asleep. And of course study their lines.

But, somehow, it all seems worthwhile as the mail for the angels pours in to the tune of 18,000 pieces a week. As far as audiences are concerned, three seems to be the winning combination.

The ringleader of this winning combination is Sabrina, lovely, svelte, and shrewd as played by veteran actress Kate Jackson. To some fans, she is the plainest of the angels, lacking the blond razzle-dazzle that Farrah has and the classic, well-chiseled beauty of Jaclyn Smith. Still, others insist that Kate has a subtle appeal, the type that springs from her quick-thinking mind and her zest for action. However, sometimes it seems as though Kate has to work harder in the role of Sabrina to create the effect that Farrah has with a flash of her smile and Jackie has with her regal beauty.

Cast and crew alike, however, marvel at Kate's spirit and nerve, some of which gets translated into tenseness on the set. "She can be tough," says one crew member. Still another executive has observed, in a half-complimentary, half-grudging note, that working with Kate is sort of like being Kissinger negotiating in the Middle East with the Arabs and the Israelis. But her years of acting experience are not for naught. She's a seasoned veteran who knows what is best for her and what works in a series.

"Sabrina is more likely to laugh than to cry," says Kate about her role. "She's tough and she spends a good deal of time thinking about consequences. I have to try and get things like that into a script."

As befitting someone of her dash and spirit, Kate's idol is another Kate—the indomitable Katharine Hepburn, great lady of stage and screen. That's the kind of acting pressure she's aiming for. Kate Jackson is a thoughtful, introspective person, certainly no lightweight in the brains department. She could have had a color TV installed in her mobile on-set retreat; instead, she had the crew build bookshelves. An avid reader with a variety of favorite authors, she especially likes fellow Southerner Lillian Hellman.

Kate was born and bred in the steel city of Birmingham, Alabama, on October 29, 1949. She is the second daughter of Hogan and Ruth Jackson, and both her parents trace their heritage for several generations back in the South. She was named just plain Kate, in honor of her grandmother, but she always wishes she had been named Katherine—which to her mind is much more aristocratic sounding.

Kate's father worked as a wholesaler of building materials while she grew up. As a child, she began carrying out her acting ambitions in the family garage, putting on skits and little plays for the kids in the neighborhood. She later graduated to a real stage when she began performing in class productions at high school in Birmingham. She continued her interest in dramatics when she went away to boarding school in Charleston, South Carolina. After high school, she attended the University of Mississippi and then switched to Birmingham Southern University as a sophomore. There she majored in drama.

Between college semesters, the Southern girl ventured up North to try her hand at summer stock. She worked at the Stowe Playhouse in Vermont for a season, as an apprentice.

Impatient to commit herself to an acting career, Kate came to New York in October 1968, when she was not yet twenty. She enrolled in the famed American Academy of Dramatic

Arts. To support herself during her studies, she held a variety of odd jobs. She worked as a tour guide for NBC, modeled wedding gowns, and sold skis. Undaunted by the brisk pace of New York City, which differed so from the unharried comfort of her native Birmingham, Kate quickly fell right into the big city groove. She shed most of her Southern drawl and began to wear bell bottom jeans, fringed poncho sweaters, and boots. No longer did she wear the tailored shirtwaists and matched coordinates that most proper Southern girls attired themselves in. She was a hip New Yorker. She admits, ''When I went home, my old friends teased me about my clothes.''

But nobody teased Kate when, just a short while after graduating from the academy in April, 1970, she landed a plum role on a daytime serial and earned her first big break. The serial was ''Dark Shadows,'' an eerie concoction of vampires and supernatural goings-on, where the plots thickened with blood and gore.

''I read for 'Dark Shadows' on a Thursday and started my role as Daphne Harridge the following Tuesday,'' she remembers. ''I was a silent ghost during the first two months on the show. I didn't have a word to say. I could watch the other professionals and learn.

''Then came my first speech, about a mile long. . . . I was doing the speech and this little kid started jumping up and down on my long gown. When I finished, I found the gown was on fire and the little trouper was stamping it out.''

''Dark Shadows'' was canceled in 1971, and Kate came out to Hollywood to try her luck. She quickly won the part of

Nurse Jill Danko on ''The Rookies.'' During her four years on the show, Kate says, ''I didn't have many big parts on that series, except when I was kidnapped, which seemed to happen a lot.'' In her final year on the cop show, Kate had grown so close to the character that she was allowed to rewrite some of what Jill said on the series. When the show was canceled, for her it was like saying good-bye to an old friend.

Ironically, the idea for ''Charlie's Angels'' was prompted by one of Kate's inspirations. Because of her popularity on ''The Rookies,'' a producer suggested that she be a star in a show about three karate-chopping molls. Kate countered with the notion that the three work for a detective. ''Then I saw a picture on the wall of three angels,'' she says. The series ''Charlie's Angels'' was born.

Perhaps the most fiercely ambitious of the three angels, Kate declares, ''It's not that I want to be an actress. I have to be an actress.

''It's not the money or the fame. It's just that I want to be somebody! If I had stayed in my home town, I could have lived and died there, and maybe nobody would have noticed me.

''I guess I want to prove that I'm alive; it's a statement that I exist. I guess I want to make waves, make some noise, and call attention to myself. Besides, being an actress is so enjoyable!''

One thing that Kate would enjoy doing is comedy, and she says that Mary Tyler Moore is one of the actresses she admires for her gift of comedy. Occasionally she jokes, with more than a bit of truth, that she'd ''like to be Mary Tyler

Moore when I grow up." But she's dead serious when she confesses that "Laverne and Shirley" is her favorite TV show and that she'd like to star in a situation comedy.

For the time being she'll concentrate on "Charlie's Angels." "I'd like to save my money and learn a lot from it," she says.

Especially now, with her once mid-back-length hair cut into a shorter, more-sophisticated style, and with the free-wheeling, independent, strong role she plays on "Charlie's Angels," Kate seems to be enjoying life and emerging into very much her own woman. She's a far cry from the young and vulnerable creature she was when she started on "The Rookies."

Yet the transition period from young adult to mature woman hasn't been easy. Kate admits to periods of confusion and frustration, especially after her long-term romance with Edward Albert broke up. Kate had dated Edward, son of actor Eddie Albert, for more than five years.

"My priorities got changed in the last six months," she confesses. "I reintroduced myself to myself. I got far away from my center. I wasn't doing what made me happy. You might say I lost Kate Jackson two years ago. I was so busy trying to please everybody else that I never had time to be alone and please myself. I like me when I feel good—which means I sleep right and do positive things for myself as well as other people."

Today there is no steady man in her life, although she does date often, especially a couple of close friends. She's not one for the Hollywood party scene, however, and would just as soon stay home with some pals and play pool. Or tinker with her photography equipment. Or head off from her high-rise apartment, with her dog Catcher in her jeep, to the mountains and deserts. Kate's learned to enjoy herself, with or without other people.

She bristles, however, at the portraits of her in recent months as being an all-work-and-no-play sort of girl, a virtual slave who does little but play tennis and go to her psychiatrist. She did say, ''I've stopped smoking and drinking and staying out late. My love life ain't what it used to be. I've just got to discipline myself or the work would just kill me.'' Yet that's all part of Kate's black humor, a tendency to overstate the case with her ripping sarcasm. The truth is that Kate, who has become used to the grueling grind of a weekly series over the years, is one of the busiest actresses on TV. She's an accomplished athlete who loves to ski and ice skate, besides playing tennis. (She once toyed with the idea of becoming a professional tennis player.) One of her favorite vacation treats is to fly to Aspen where she indulges in downhill and cross-country skiing. She also enjoys fishing and horseback riding and has been taking flying lessons.

She's into music too, and plays the guitar and dabbles a little on the piano. Traveling is also high on her list of activities.

Th only angel who has never been married, Kate doesn't discount the idea of marriage in her life. She talks about the warmth of family life and the treasured closeness she had as a child with her older sister Jenny and her mother and father. She would like to get married and have children, but for now, those goals are in the distant future. For someone as busy as she is with her work, Kate feels that now is not the time to raise a family. And she would rather not be one of those actresses who have guilt pangs every time they must leave their toddlers for the studio.

Of course, if Kate had stayed in Birmingham, like most of her childhood chums, she realizes that by now she would have been a wife and mother. But she acknowledges that acting came first.

"I thought of marriage of course, but I always knew I wanted to be an actress," she says simply, and without a trace of regret.

It was ballet and not acting that lured angel Jaclyn Smith away from her hometown of Houston, Texas, to show business and New York. Ever since she was three years old, Jackie, as her friends call her, wanted to be a ballerina and follow in the fluttery footsteps of world famous ballerina Margot Fonteyn.

"My whole show business career started when I was just three years old. My parents gave me a pair of pink satin ballet shoes and that was the beginning. I knew then that dancing would always be part of my life," says Jackie thoughtfully.

Like Kelly Garrett, her angel character, Jackie was born (on October 26, 1947) and raised in Texas. Her parents are Jack and Margaret Ellen Smith, whom she calls "the sweetest people in the world." She is the younger of two children and her father is a dentist.

Very much the old-fashioned girl, the kind whose rigid moral standards make her think "heck" is a foul word, Jackie remains very close to her parents today. Although she is almost thirty, she still considers herself "their little girl."

"I guess when you are a child and you receive so much

love, you have an awful lot to give later on. I had that love then and I still have it now,'' she says.

The love and affection that Jackie received from her parents was also demonstrated as support for her creative endeavors. Both her mother and father always encouraged her in her work, whether it was ballet or acting, which she began to dabble in as a student at Pershing Junior High School in Houston. Jackie began working there with the local community playhouse.

Despite her talents, she maintains she was shy and not very popular. ''I was strictly a wallflower, though my mother would never admit it,'' she admits. ''But the fact is I didn't relate very well in school. Ballet was the only thing that occupied my mind.''

After graduation from Lamar High School, Jackie enrolled at Trinity University in San Antonio. She dropped out after a year of acute homesickness and thinking about ballet all the time.

Mustering up her courage, Jackie, like fellow angel Kate Jackson, migrated north to New York. She settled into the Barbizon Hotel for Women with an allowance of $1,000 a month from her father. She landed a few roles in some musicals and one of these led to work in commercials. First came a Listerine ad, then a Diet-Rite, then Camay, and soon Jackie was one of the most sought-after models in New York, earning well over $100,000 a year.

But despite the money which poured in from commercials, she did not forsake her interest in dancing. In fact, she organized a ballet class under the auspices of the Head Start program for underprivileged children. Although she has given up the idea of becoming a professional ballerina —because she says she doesn't have the emotional dedication—she still continues to practice daily.

It was while Jackie was out on a modeling call that she met actor Roger Davis, the man who was overwhelmed by her beauty and who would later marry her. Roger, of "Dark Shadows" and "Alias Smith and Jones" fame, noticed her sitting in a reception room waiting for an interview. He thought she was the most exquisite creature he had ever seen. He arranged for a friend to introduce them, and soon after they started dating, they were wed.

Sadly, the marriage broke up after five years, although Jackie insists that she remains on the best of terms with her ex-husband. However, the breakup is still somewhat distressing to her. She will admit, wistfully, that she had hoped to have a large brood of children by now.

"Nothing would please me more than to marry tomorrow," she reveals, although she says it's hard to find a man with the same kind of moral beliefs she has. "I'm dying to have kids, but you can't rush into marriage just for the sake of being married. I'd like to meet someone who thinks like I do. It isn't easy."

Although Jackie's modeling career was extensive, her acting experience before "Charlie's Angels" was light. She had a small role in the movie *The Adventurers*, and parts in prime-time series like "McCloud" and "The Rookies" and "Get Christie Love."

Jackie is quiet and subdued and is a sharp contrast on the "Angels" set to whimsical Farrah and outspoken Kate. She admits that she's a loner who enjoys spending time off by herself practicing her ballet. Her best friend of all is her bouncy black poodle Albert.

Those who penetrate behind the quiet veneer and get close to Jackie say she's a deeply emotional and sensitive person who has strong ties to home and family and is very sentimental. Perhaps the home where she lives in Beverly Hills is an indication of this. It's a large twelve-room mansion with pillars, much like *Gone with the Wind*'s Tara estate, the kind of home you'd imagine for a real Southern belle. In Jackie's bedroom is an old-fashioned, brass-canopied bed, covered with flouncy pillows and a thick white bedspread. Although she says she bought the house with investment in mind, it's obvious that she enjoys the solitude and comfort that it gives her.

Subdued and reserved she may be, but Jackie becomes most enthusiastic when she talks about "Charlie's Angels."

"It's really a terrific feeling being pampered the way we are on "Charlie's Angels." I love playing Kelly Garrett on the series and the girls are terrific to work with. . . . Then there's the fan mail. A lot of women write to me. Some want photos to give to their husbands."

But again, revealing her ingrained traditional streak, she says she'd chuck it all in a minute if the right man came along. The fame and fortune she's reaped from "Charlie's Angels" are nice, but love and children would be even nicer as far as Jackie is concerned. Again, that's where her old-fashioned streak comes into play. She would feel most fulfilled being a wife and a mother.

"I bet many people would think I'm crazy to think about my personal future when my career is going so great," acknowledges Jackie with a toss of her thick chestnut hair. "I'm normal and healthy and I guess it's because I've been modeling for many years that a career isn't important. Sure, things are going great, I would like to have the best of both worlds, but if it came down to the fact that I had to choose one . . . well, don't tempt me.

"I miss Texas," she adds. "I miss my family and friends. Life is lived at a slower and less hectic pace in Houston. I guess I'm something of an old-fashioned girl. I don't like a lot of contemporary movies. I've discovered it's important to leave your work behind you for some quiet moments alone to maintain your peace of mind. Whenever Hollywood becomes too much for me, I dance around the living room to clear my head."

Her closeness with her own parents and sister and the abundance of love she felt as a child contribute to her need for a family. Today her parents are extremely proud of her, and they often let their famous daughter know how much they respect her success. To them it's hardly a surprise that Jackie should be playing on a top-rated show. Yet she says they're very "unpretentious and down to earth" and don't brag all the time to other people about her.

Tha kind of pride and closeness is what Jackie looks forward to having in her own family. The giving and the caring and the growth and, above all, the fun. "It's really the only way when you get down to it, isn't it?" she'll ask rhetorically.

Jackie's old-fashioned–girl core and the effect of her Methodist minister grandfather ("the strongest influence in my life," she calls him) show up in her personal habits. She doesn't drink hard liquor and doesn't smoke. She doesn't spice up her conversation with racy four-letter words.

Off the set, besides her dancing, Jackie enjoys sports like swimming, water skiing, and horseback riding. She also plays tennis a little. Music is another one of her hobbies and the rooms of her Southern-styled mansion, decorated with beautiful and valuable antiques, are often filled with the strains of classical music.

Not one for the party scene, Jackie enjoys a simple evening out, like dining on pizza or Mexican food and then taking in a movie.

Jackie takes her stardom in stride, pleased at her tremendous success with "Charlie's Angels" but at the same time not overwhelmed by it. She's a serene type who doesn't allow herself to be affected by superstardom. "I was happy before the show," she declares easily. "I'm happy now, and if it stopped tomorrow, I'd still be happy."

David Doyle, who plays John Bosley on the series, confesses that he was happy before the series too, but now, as far as he's concerned, it's like having his dreams come true. Not just because "Charlie's Angels" is a top-rated hit that has zoomed to the top of the ratings. But also because David is working alongside three of the most gorgeous women in the world.

As David confesses, "When I was a twenty-year-old apprentice at the Barter Theater in Virginia, I used to fantasize about acting in Hollywood, surrounded by the most beautiful women on earth."

Well, now it's twenty-six years later, and Doyle is forty-six and most happily married for the past eight years. But that doesn't mean he can't enjoy the good fortune of appearing in a weekly series surrounded by lovelies like Farrah, Kate, and Jaclyn. His only regret is that it didn't happen sooner, when he was in his twenties, but better late than never.

Of course, Doyle admits with an impish smile, if he were single, things would be different around the set of "Charlie's Angels." He notes that the single gals on the show, Kate and Jaclyn, seem to spend a lot of spare time with their canine pets. Doyle contends that if he were a free man, he'd make sure those dogs had some competition for their owner's attentions. He'd make sure that Kate and Jaclyn spent time with someone more sophisticated and debonair. Someone like himself.

Doyle has nothing but glowing praise for his three costars, and it doesn't ruffle his acting ego that he has to share acting honors with a trio of women. He not only appreciates their beauty, but also respects their intelligence and their sophistication. He feels that's the reason the show has succeeded so phenomenally.

Like his beautiful co-workers, Doyle also has to take up new disguises each week, in the course of his undercover assignments.

"I tape them all," he explains. "By the time the season ends, I'll have fifty or sixty different roles on tape. For instance, the other day Farrah and I pretended we were out of the cow country, driving a big ol' car with steer horns on the front. I said, 'I feel as low as gully dirt.' How often do you get to say a line like that?"

There's only one thing that troubles Doyle about working with his angels: he thinks Farrah and Jackie spend too much time brushing their hair, worrying about the way it looks, even when it will get easily messed up anyway in a chase scene. Kate had her hair specially cut for the show into a chin-length, layered hairdo, the kind that falls readily into place with a few quick shakes of her head. Brushing is hardly necessary for her. But Farrah and Jackie, who have done many commercials for hair products, are always scrupulous about having their tresses in perfect place.

Doyle knows the girls must look beautiful, even in the most hair-raising of scenes, but he admits that the hairbrushing drives him crazy. He's often thought, as a joke, of buying little brushes for himself and the male crew members. Then, just as a scene was to be filmed, he would yell "Wait!" and would then proceed to arrange his hair.

But that's the only source of irritation that David Doyle finds about the devastating trio he shepherds, as Bosley, to their dangerous assignments. And he'd be the first to confess that "the girls probably wouldn't look as good with crew cuts!"

Hairbrushing aside, Doyle finds that he's in seventh heaven working with his angelic threesome, just like the millions of viewers who find the series out of this world. And some 40 percent of the people in the country, who eagerly tune in each week to see these delectable detectives ferret out crime, just can't be wrong!

Off the court Farrah may joke and clown around, but on the court, she's one of the most formidable tennis players in Hollywood.

A girl who likes to dress well, Farrah's got two mink coats and is thinking of adding a sable to her collection.

Richard Anderson (right) sends The Six Million Dollar Man, better known as Lee Majors, out on those dangerous top-secret missions.

Lindsay Wagner, as the Bionic Woman, captured the heart of Lee Majors on "The Six Million Dollar Man."

Lee does a little bionic arm wrestling with heavyweight champion Muhammed Ali.

A talented athlete, Farrah enjoys most any kind of sport, from golf to gymnastics.

Farrah co-stars with Kate Jackson and Jaclyn Smith in "Charlie's Angels," the hottest show on TV this season.

9

It's true. Farrah Fawcett is not only beautiful, she's also nice. And what's more, she's very happy. If you think that Farrah has just about everything, she'd be the first to agree with you. There are no deep-seated problems or troubling anxieties that plague her. As far as she's concerned, life couldn't be better.

That's why Farrah has been accused of being a Pollyanna, cockeyed optimist, a persistent viewer of the world through rose-colored glasses. People have said that her cheerful and bouncy demeanor is a front, that there lurks behind her blond buoyancy a whole kit and kaboodle of typical actress's neuroses, problems, and hang-ups.

But the truth is that Farrah *is* happy, and relatively free from the mental turmoil that seems to beset most of her peers in her chosen profession. In a country where a lot of people spend a lot of time on analysts' couches sorting out the reasons for their despair, Farrah feels that her existence is nothing less than truly blessed.

"I couldn't be happier with my life," she chirps. "I love Lee, I love my family, my house, my dogs—Texas. That's why whenever anyone wants to interview me, I think, 'Why? It's so dull.'

"Sometimes," she confesses, with a mischievous twinkle in those heavenly gray green eyes, "I wish I could be like some of the actresses I've read about. Going to psychiatrists all the time. Having a hard time in life. That kind of thing. But I'm not that way, I'm just a normal person with a nice kind of life."

And Farrah is a nice kind of person. Girls who are consumed with jealousy when they meet this blond bundle of gorgeousness are rather pleasantly surprised to find that there's not a mean bone or one streak of egomania in her lean, athletic body. She's kind and sweet with a marvelously witty sense of humor. People who want to hate her for the wonderful way she looks, who try desperately to find some tragic flaw in her personality, come away convinced that Farrah is just as fabulous inside as she is outside.

Farrah attributes her sunny outlook toward life on being an Aquarius. It makes her cheerful and optimistic, she declares. And there's also the fact that Farrah has her head screwed on right. She's got a healthy perspective of what's important in life—and what's not important. And she lives by the philosophy that whatever happens, happens. She's not going to agonize over the future, nor will she fret about what transpired in the past. She's glad she's an up-and-coming actress, one of the most popular on today's TV and movie screen, but she refuses to worry about how long it's going to last. What really matters to her is her family—her mother, her father, Lee, her sister. She's not driven to claw her way to the top. Being a world famous star is something Farrah could easily do without; her main concerns above everything else are her home and her loved ones. That's why hardly anything can set her tousled mane on end; that's why her dander never gets up.

"I have the philosophy that what is going to happen is going to happen," she explains. "In other words, I really don't have control over my life. Things were set for me long ago."

But that doesn't mean that Farrah falls into the stereotype of a dumb blonde. On the contrary, she's a quick-witted girl with a ready barrage of funny comments. She surprises people who expect someone who looks as good as she does to be totally lacking in brain power. More than once a producer or director has said to her, "We thought you were a dumb blonde—beautiful but nothing going on upstairs!"

While acknowledging that her looks have certainly been more of a help than a drawback, and have caused her to get her foot in the door of many acting studios, Farrah will still sigh and say, "It's the old Marilyn Monroe syndrome. Nobody takes a pretty girl seriously."

Most of the time, though, Farrah is busy counting her blessings, and appreciating the fact that her tawny tigress-style beauty has earned her several hundreds of thousands of dollars a year in acting and modeling fees. She enjoys the high sums of money she reaps from her work and relishes spending as much as she does working. With the booty she's collected from her various assignments, Farrah's bought two mink coats, closets full of expensive, chic clothes, and other beautiful possessions. If someone would accuse her of being mercenary, that doesn't bother her, because she feels that she works too hard in show business not to be paid well and to enjoy her rewards.

"Money comes first," she asserts. "You work too hard in this business not to be paid well."

With her newfound stardom in her role on "Charlie's Angels," Farrah's contemplating another luxurious purchase for herself—a sable coat. The price tag for these opulent furs, for a full-length coat, runs somewhere between $30,000 and $70,000. In the meantime, however, she'll content herself with shopping at some of the exclusive boutiques around Hollywood. Like the fancy Pickwick Fashions store in Sherman Oaks, California, where she went on a shopping spree that cost her some $1,500, "for a few things to tide me over the holidays." Farrah likes tailored, well-cut clothes, and one of her favorite purchases was a hacking jacket suit.

But a handsome and well-heeled wardrobe isn't the only esthetic pleasure for Farrah. Time and again, she has declared that her first love, above acting and modeling, is art. Farrah is an accomplished sculptress and painter, who could easily chuck all the fame and glory of being a glamorous Charlie's Angel and return contentedly to her marble and her chisel.

The Fawcett-Majors country-style French home in Bel Air is decorated with many of Farrah's inspired creations. She's not merely a celebrity artist, but a talented and gifted designer who could probably earn a good living with her works. Several years ago, she sold a stone-cast, life-size torso for $3,500, and more recently a connoisseur picked up a sepia sketch by Farrah for $250. Lately, however, Lee has not been willing for his wife to auction off her creations. He's more than willing to match any offered price to keep her compositions at home where he believes they belong.

"I just haven't the time to do as much as I'd like," sighs Farrah. "I'm flattered when someone wants to buy any of my pieces, but Lee refuses to let it go. 'I'll pay you exactly what you'd get from anyone else,' he says. Someday when my show business career is over, and I'm home with my children, I'll devote long hours to sculpting.

"Sculpting is the most gratifying thing I have ever done," she continues. "I am amazed to see what I can create from a piece of clay with my hands and my imagination."

Another thing Farrah loves to create is luscious gourmet meals in the kitchen. Even after a hard day of rehearsing and filming, Farrah enjoys whipping this and mixing that to come up with a menu that would do justice to any discriminating palate. It's not that she feels tied to the kitchen; it's simply that as a Southern girl bred on good home cooking, she's simply crazy about cooking. Whether it's a fancy concoction for dessert or a simple recipe like chocolate chip cookies, she likes working in the kitchen. Now that her career is mushrooming and the demands of filming leave her little opportunity for gourmet experiments, she's been forced to give up much of her cooking and hire a housekeeper to prepare meals.

It's one of the ways her life has changed since she became Farrah the superstar. She has gone from being just a beautiful face in hair commercials to one of the most popular and famous actresses around; but Farrah had not counted on some of the fallout effects when she was a youngster growing up in Corpus Christi, Texas.

"I didn't realize this would be so time-consuming," she'll exclaim, after an exhausting day before the cameras, stretching out her lean and limber body in a comfortable chair. "Somebody's always at you for something. But what do you say to a woman who has been waiting since 6:30 in the morning for an autograph—go away?

"I always thought they did it for you. When I was a girl fantasizing about movie stars, I thought all the problems were handled by somebody else. Wardrobe, for instance—I thought they'd bring in 500 dresses and all you'd have to do is point.

"Boy," she says, flashing one of her brilliant grins which display thirty-six perfect teeth, "was I wrong!"

Explaining how the life of a Charlie's angel is not all heavenly, Farrah once said, "Lee comes home at night, has a sandwich and shower, and flops into bed. I do women's work. I take off my nail polish, figure out a menu for tomorrow, maybe clean a room. In the morning I get up an hour and a half earlier than Lee and clean and get food ready and do half a dozen other chores. I've done a lot of work by the time the limousine rolls up at 5:30."

Still, Farrah feels that things are so fantastic for her now that she can hardly complain. Although stardom sort of fell into her lap, she obviously relishes its benefits. The fact that she didn't arrive in Hollywood all set and eager and compelled to make it to the top probably makes her swift success seem all the more wonderful. It was all so unexpected.

"It's very gratifying to give a good performance and you can't say, 'Gee, it's not wonderful having that 90 percent of the fans come up and say wonderful things to you.' Forget about the 10 percent who don't! I think any actress who says she doesn't enjoy herself that way is lying to herself —because it *is* great and it makes me happy and my parents happy. I get a great deal of satisfaction out of that."

Farrah also gets a great deal of satisfaction out of being a woman. Clearly, she feels that women have the edge over men in this world. Although she thinks that the male animal of the human species is stronger, she feels that there are other gifts which women have that more than compensate. As far as she's concerned, women have a better deal in this life.

"Any woman who says she doesn't use her femininity to get what she wants is deceiving herself. Men don't have our instinct and we don't have their strength.

"I'd say we got a lot more, so I really can't complain," she says with a demure grin.

Yet when it comes to strength in athletics, Farrah is most definitely a formidable opponent who's been known to make even her superjock husband Lee slink away in defeat. She's a crackerjack tennis player and a golfer who shoots in the low nineties. She also enjoys hunting (Lee had her accompany him on a quail-hunting expedition just last year in Oklahoma), fishing, water skiing, snow skiing, and many other sports. When she's not hacking away at a new piece of marble in her sculpture studio, she's shamming away at the ball over the tennis court net, with a vigor that could match the likes of Billie Jean King and Chris Evert.

Lee plays a lot of tennis and golf with his lovely spouse, although he readily confesses that he won't join her for a slalom down the ski slopes again. It's all because of one episode when Farrah clearly outshone him.

''I'm up there on the top of the hill, trying to stand up, doin' my little bunny number, you know, the snow plow, and here she comes by, zip, zip. It really got to me. I've never been back on skis since,'' he admits with a sheepish grin.

Farrah, like so many other California girls, is a water baby and loves the fact that she and Lee live close to the ocean. She loves picnics on the sand and running up and down the beach barefoot, especially early in the morning when it's lonely and fresh.

Her love of the outdoors also extends to gardening. She enjoys puttering around the flower beds in her Bel Air home and has cultivated a crop of fresh vegetables, which often land on the Fawcett-Majors dinner table.

Despite her beauty and her awe-inspiring array of talents, Farrah confesses that in her Southern heart, she is ''a very shy person basically.'' That's one of the reasons why she never attended acting school. She just felt too embarrassed to step in front of an entire class and act. She joined an acting class once and the experience was traumatic. For once, Farrah's usually placid feathers were ruffled.

She was ordered to stand up in front of the whole class and pretend that she was a growing musnroom. Embarrassed, afraid, shy, unsure, Farrah refused to do it. She thought the entire thing was silly. She became hysterical and left the class. She never returned—and never joined another acting class.

Obviously her lack of formal training in acting hasn't stifled her career. Critics have noted that Farrah displays a remarkable gift for comedy, that she has the good timing and sprightly sense to become a natural comedienne.

But no matter how far Farrah will go in Hollywood—and her future is probably the brightest among all the up-and-coming actresses—her heart will always belong to Texas. "Texans are great," she exclaims, with a good share of native state pride.

When Farrah and Lee travel to the Lone Star State for one of their informal, short vacations, she slips into that deep country drawl, a thick Southwestern accent that she fought so hard to get rid of when she first came to Hollywood. Barely a trace of it remains today in her everyday speech, but it still returns in full Dixie flavor when she and Lee have an intimate chat at home.

"Even today, I still say 'ah' instead of 'I,' " she explains, although her voice hardly reveals a trace of the drawl that she claims to have in offhand moments. "And when I'm very excited or sad, my accent returns in all its glory. I'm constantly aware of it because when I go home to Lee at night, he has a noticeable Kentucky-type accent and it's probably contagious."

Farrah's devotion to her parents and her hometown is typical of her old-fashioned sentimentality and values. She and Lee go to Texas often, at least three or four times a year. Farrah enjoys the visits, especially since it gives her a chance to get away from the tinsel-world atmosphere of Hollywood and come back to her real roots. Being in Texas, surrounded by her family and the land where she grew up, Farrah comes to grips with who she really is. Sometimes that concept is difficult to grasp in California, where she's one of the fast-rising stars of a new generation of celebrities. But when she goes back to Texas, she gets a handle on herself. She doesn't have to be glamorous or sophisticated or anything else. She can just be Farrah, the little girl from Corpus Christi who made it big.

Superstardom hasn't caused a superego to sprout inside of Farrah's head. She's still very much the Texas belle, the girl-next-door who radiates sweetness and niceness—in Hollywood, the town where those values are all but forgotten. She's fast becoming the personality of the decade, but all she says about it is that the whole thing is "neat."

"I don't see myself as anybody special. And I don't really understand all the interest," she declares, in the face of overwhelming popularity.

Modestly, she explains that the one major effect stardom has had on her life is that she can't do the marketing anymore because she immediately gets engulfed with hordes of adoring fans. Otherwise, Farrah has remained unchanged by all the hulabaloo. It may be her dazzling smile and bathing-suited figure that graces the best-selling poster in history, but Farrah remains sweet Farrah.

A case in point demonstrates this. A young girl who was the niece of a crew member of "Charlie's Angels" wanted to interview Farrah for her school paper. Farrah, despite the heavy demands of press the country over, decided to oblige. The day the girl arrived on the set, Farrah was as usual surrounded by people—makeup artists, agents, producers, directors, the customary entourage for a star. But when she was told that her junior interviewer had arrived, Farrah quickly excused herself and went over to the girl. It was just another example of Farrah's warmhearted hospitality and refreshing down-to-earthness.

Perhaps the basic Farrah is best described in a joke told by comic Carl Reiner, who's known and liked the silver-streaked superstar for many years. "She told me she was mad at her maid, but knew how to get even," quips Reiner. "I asked her how. She said, 'I'm not going to fix her hair anymore!' "

Yes, Farrah Fawcett is as nice as she is beautiful. She's every bit as sweet as she looks. When asked to reveal her worst vice, Farrah wrinkled her brow and thought for a few minutes. Then, flashing that trademark grin, she said, "Eating too many Cheetos!"

Like Farrah, her husband Lee Majors also has a zingy and perky sense of humor, which is rarely displayed on "The Six Million Dollar Man." Also, because Lee has a touch of that country shyness and reserve, he's not known to be a funny-man at parties. So when he comes out with a witty one-liner out of the blue, it seems unexpected and contrary to form. But Lee definitely has a lighter side. When he was working on the "Owen Marshall" show, the cast and crew were riddled with nervousness. The show's star, Arthur Hill, was described by an observer as being "pretty uptight." But when Lee would start kidding around, everybody, including Hill, would relax.

When Lee first came to Hollywood. there was hardly any

humor in this serious and earnest young man. As a matter of fact, he had a reputation for brashness and rudeness—the proud and arrogant newcomer who was predicting that he would have an Oscar nomination in less than ten years. His friends now say that all that was just a cover-up for shyness, and that over the years, he's mellowed. Particularly through his own maturity and his relationship with Farrah. After a hard day of fighting crime as TV's bionic man, Lee likes nothing better than to spend a quiet evening with his beautiful wife—whom he proclaims as The Most Beautiful Woman in the World.

Despite his stardom, Lee is very much the simple boy from Kentucky. He defines the good things in life, not as yachts or Rolls Royces, but as having enough time to go fishing and hunting. The home he shares with Farrah in Bel Air has enough land to indulge Lee's love of animals—they keep a horse and three dogs, including an Afghan.

One of his favorite sports and pastimes is a game of flag football with a group of friends on the weekends. That's a game in which the players have two cloth streamers tied around their waists—the opponents must grab the streamers of the guy with the ball.

"It's kind of like a touch football game, but some of those teams are awfully rough," explains Lee. "In fact, last year, we had a couple of ex-Rams players with us. So it's a pretty good brand of football even though it's what you call flag. I mean to grab the flag of a guy coming at you at ninety miles per hour is pretty tough."

The kind of actor who shuns the jet-setting, party-going life, Lee boasts that "our house is our family." When he and

Farrah do go out, it's usually for a quiet dinner with friends like Johnny Carson and Dinah Shore and Sonny Bono, rather than a gala premiere. Publicity is one thing he can easily do without. As a former press agent once said about Lee, only half kidding, ''He pays me to keep his name out of the papers.''

But there are some sides of stardom that gratify Lee immensely. Like the time in 1968 when he was in Hubert Humphrey's hotel suite for the election. The shy boy from Kentucky was awed by the whole thing. ''That was history in the making. It was stimulating!'' he exclaims.

But the kind of publicity that really turns Lee off is gossip about his private life—especially about him and Farrah.

And when things get rough, when the pressure becomes too great or the stories get too irritating, he and Farrah can always escape to the retreat that Lee has owned for several years in Arizona, on Lake Meade. ''It's out in the middle of nowhere, I kind of hide out there,'' says Lee. There's a boat and a jeep and just plain country solitude for the couple who delight in each other's company so much.

You can take the boy out of the country, but you can never take the country out of the boy. After Lee landed his first TV role on ''The Big Valley,'' he moved into a small ranch house in Malibu, California, near the Pacific Ocean. In addition to his work on the TV series, Lee was happy to work on the ranch as a caretaker for $100 a month. No fancy high-rise apartments or stuffy mansions for him. He liked the free and easy style of a ranch. After a few more years of success, Lee was able to buy the house he was tending. He kept a menagerie of three horses, six dogs, a burro, and a pet raccoon at one time on the ranch, and got along splendidly with them all. He far preferred their company to some of the jazzy names in Hollywood.

But despite his occasional desire to be alone, Lee still counts among his friends some of the biggest names in Hollywood. He's very close to Burt Reynolds and predicts with friendly pride that "Burt will eventually become one of our big giants."

He's also fond of John Wayne, whom he met on a flight from Los Angeles to Australia. "He's a heck of a man," admires Lee.

Lee's own penchant for alcohol comes in the form of margueritas, the salt-laced drink made with tequila. It's a long and sophisticated way from the time when he was a kid in Kentucky where, as Lee recalls, "You'd put a dollar on a stump out in the woods, come back an hour later and there'd be a Mason jar full of white lightnin'." He's also fond of good, American-style food, and even contemplated opening up a restaurant in Los Angeles. The kind of items Lee would feature on the menu are some of his own favorites—like buffalo steak, and New England prawns fried in beer batter.

Farrah gobbles down cookies by the dozens and Cheetos by the bag and still frets about losing ten pounds because the hectic pace of the series has taken its toll. "I eat everything I can get my hands on," she sighs, "and I'm still dropping poundage. Working so long each day just melts the weight off.

"Of course Lee has the other problem—he must watch what he eats or he'll balloon up."

So, for now, for those weekday nights when Lee and Farrah curl up together in front of their TV set in the bedroom—just like millions of other couples across America—Lee will restrain himself from snacking. While Farrah happily munches away on some cookies, Lee abstains, in hopes of maintaining his six million dollar form. The junk foods are for Farrah, and Lee will simply lean back against his pillow and watch TV, in his favorite room in the house. The bedroom is decorated in Lee's favorite colors of deep forest green, tan, and brown. It's well furnished but very comfortable.

Among the shows they like to watch are each other's series, but Farrah will admit, "We watch his more. He kind of falls asleep in mine. But I love his show. I never really think he's bad. I'm still a lot of notches behind him as an actress."

A shrewd man with money who believes in putting away for that rainy day, Lee has wisely invested in other ventures with the heady sums he's received from television. He has a dry cleaning business in Ohio and some oil wells in Oklahoma and Kansas. He may be close to a multimillionaire, but Lee doesn't like to waste money. He never spends lavishly.

Another sideline Lee is interested in is music. He plays the guitar very well and has composed hundreds of songs. Perhaps one day he might make an investment in some area of the music business.

One area where Lee is reluctant to tread is television talk shows, although friends have said that with his ready banter and deft quips, he'd be a big hit. But Lee refuses to appear, even with emcees like friends Dinah Shore, Merv Griffin, Mike Douglas, and Johnny Carson.

"I don't do talk shows," he says simply and flatly. "I don't do talk shows because I'm an actor and I feel that most of the times when you do talk shows, you're at the mercy of the interviewer. . . . Unless I felt I could really contribute to a show, I'd rather not put myself in that position.

"Unless you're a singer or a comedian, you come off looking dumb."

For one thing, Lee doesn't even like to get dressed up. He's far more at ease in jeans and a T-shirt than in a dinner jacket. When he first came to Hollywood, he didn't even own a suit. Now that it's written into his contract that he receives the clothes he wears on the series at the end of the season, he spends less and less time shopping.

"I guess it's just that I don't lead the kind of life in Hollywood that calls for a wardrobe," he says honestly. "My life is outdoors and I dress accordingly."

He cheerfully admits that he went years before owning a dinner jacket—usually a prime requisite for stars who make personal appearances. His first one was purchased for him by producer Aaron Spelling. Spelling bought it for Lee to make personal appearances with the ABC-TV movie, *Ballad of Andy Crocker*. "He also threw in a fifty-dollar pair of shoes, formal shirt, tie, and gold studs," laughs Lee.

There are good points about both spouses starring in top-rate series. When Farrah was just modeling, Lee would arrive home from a back-breaking day of bionic duties, tired and barely able to move. Farrah would want to go out. Now Farrah's as tired as Lee is at the end of the day.

"Lee says he's glad I got the series," giggled Farrah, "because it means when he comes home at night, I don't say—'We're going out tonight.' "

Being home alone with Farrah is what Lee likes more than anything else in the world. And with a home like the one he shares with his angelic wife in Bel Air, it's no wonder that he finds it such a pleasant retreat from the Hollywood neon. It's a spacious, three-bedroom house, decorated in a French-country style. It has a warm and intimate style in spite of its tremendous space—about 8,000 square feet. There are tennis courts and a pool.

Although it's furnished in a style that would do justice to any home decorating magazine, the Majors home has the kind of easygoing air that makes it very comfortable, in spite of the richness of the surroundings. Some of the walls have been upholstered in doeskin suede, to absorb exterior sound and loud noises. There are many fireplaces and lots of her-ringbone brick and hardwood floors. Farrah's got a beautiful dressing room designed for her in her favorite colors of peach, green, and tan. There are chairs in the dressing room for friends or Lee to chat with her as she makes the transfor-mation, with the help of a few cosmetics, from being beauti-ful to simply breathtaking.

When he's not relaxing in his Bel Air abode, Lee likes to play one of his favorite sports. He really likes to hunt but complains, "When I'm off the series, the hunting season is off too. But that's what I grew up doing—hunting and fishing. And of course golf is something that's come along in the last three or four years for me. Farrah plays a lot of tennis, so I have to play enough to appease her. But I really prefer golf.''

Lee's love of the putting game is so great that he has been known to wind up a busy on-location filming session by heading straight from the airport to the golf course.

The insecure, nervous, and timid young man from Kentucky is a thing of the past, a relic from the bygone sixties. When Lee first came out to Hollywood, he was shaky about his career and had the feeling that the earth might crumble under his feet at any minute. He was afraid that he might dissolve into anonymity at any moment. To insure his future, Lee didn't give up his job with the parks department for several years after his debut with ''The Big Valley.''

But now that Lee Majors has gone forever. A new Lee Majors has bloomed, thanks to a starring role in one of TV's most popular series, and a glamorous and successful wife.

After all, the record speaks for itself. In contrast to other actors and actresses, who started out over a decade ago and are now only mentioned in guess-whatever-happened-to–type questions from time to time, Lee has never been without an acting job.

''I've worked in this town a dozen years and in four series,'' says Lee.

''It's kind of unbelievable,'' he adds, acknowledging that his track rate, while not bionic, is certainly phenomenal. ''I've been so fortunate. . . . I've never really been out of work. I've been in one series after another—'The Big Valley,' 'The Men from Shiloh,' 'Owen Marshal,' and 'The Six Million Dollar Man.' ''

Maybe it has something to do with Lee's hulking figure, his well-built good looks, the fact that he's a sandy-haired blond with blue eyes and 175 pounds distributed over a six-foot frame. But mostly it has something to do with Lee's dedication, the fact that as a child he set out to make his adoptive parents proud of him. The drive to success was nurtured very early on in Lee Majors' life and obviously it has paid off handsomely.

And Farrah has succeeded too, most likely because of a great inner sense of security and love that was given her as a child. As sweet and pleasant as she is, she also knows very much what she wants and what is good for her. That's why, although she's not yet thirty, she's learned to rely on her own judgment and trust her instincts. That's one of the reasons Farrah is such a mixed bag of tricks. On the one hand she's traditional and conservative, a wife first and career-girl second. On the other hand, she knows her own mind and is very conscious of what she should do.

But nobody can tell her what to do or push her around. ''I'm stronger than I look,'' she states. ''I do not intend to be pushed around—particularly not by any press agent who wants me to look like something I'm not.''

She loves to cuddle up with Lee and listen to romantic music by a fireplace or on a cozy couch. But she also likes a good healthy fight to clear the air between her and her husband. She's always said she couldn't stand being married to a man who would agree with her totally. And she knows Lee would not want just a "Yes, sir" wife around either.

Practically fearless, especially when it comes to athletic competitions, Farrah has one thing that makes her anxious. She's bothered by fans who trail her in cars. She's always a little unsure about whether they're harmless or some kind of dangerous nuts.

But generally she's flashing that heavenly smile and is pretty implacable and serene. In that respect she's a contrast to Lee, who can be moody and quiet at times.

"I'm always up, and sometimes I'll say to him, 'You're a big grumphead!' " Farrah admits.

She swears it's all part of her Texan heritage. After all, that's the way women like her are brought up in that state.

"Southern girls are not as aggressive," explains Farrah. "California and New York girls come on very strong. Southern girls are taught differently—you get more by going the other way. New York girls may be small and beautifully boned, but city life makes them very pushy. Ever try to beat one out of a taxi? I remember being in New York with my mother and hailing a cab. After I finally got one to stop, a seventy-year-old woman stepped ahead of us. . . ."

Farrah is the kind of woman who was never driven to achieve all this success and fame in the first place; her amused husband maintains that she would choose a high-fashion-magazine cover portrait over an Oscar anyday. If the pressure gets too great, if the stakes become too high, if the pace becomes too frantic, Farrah will simply cut out. It wouldn't be that hard for her to chuck it all and leave the acting business forever. Because she'd really be just as happy baking and cooking, sculpting and painting, being a good wife and becoming a wonderful mother.

Who wouldn't want to look like Farrah Fawcett-Majors?
Who wouldn't want to have that cascading mane of golden
hair? Who wouldn't want to have her gorgeous, peachy-
colored skin and that smile of stunningly perfect teeth?
Farrah's dazzling beauty is a combination of schoolgirl innocence and womanliness. She's the girl-next-door and the
sophisticated *femme fatale* all rolled into one. She also has
the kind of pizzazz and presence that ignites a room full of
people. Many actresses have stunning features and well-
chiseled looks, but few have the kind of breathtaking
glamour that flashing-eyed Farrah has.

It helps, of course, to be naturally endowed with beauty,
and born with the kind of face that looks like a dream. But
Farrah does cultivate her looks. Like most highly paid models, she's acquired a long list of tips and secrets through the

years for looking her best. Those are the hints that make this Charlie's angel look so heavenly.

Farrah's most outstanding beauty characteristic is undoubtedly her hair, clipped in the long, layered style which is her trademark. It's a long, loosely curled style that caresses her shoulders in a just-barely messed way. Her hair looks so natural, but the truth is that Farrah works hard to achieve this look. Her uncurled, unset hair is a far cry from the golden mane with which she zips through the episodes of ''Charlie's Angels.''

''My hair is naturally curly,'' explains Farrah, confessing what really goes on when the rollers and the hairdresser aren't around. ''Not frizzy, exactly—but very full. But it's not glamorous and gorgeous—it's not the style I'm known for.''

To demonstrate that this is not just an example of Farrah's Southern modesty, she tells a story about what happened when she had a sauna bath with a friend and then let her hair go *au naturel*. After the sauna, Farrah didn't bother to have her hair reset. Instead she dashed out to do some grocery shopping with her hair frizzy, and sort of lank and droopy. She looked more like a candidate for a Raggedy Ann doll than a Charlie's angel.

In the supermarket, a fan saw Farrah's hair, went through a few seconds of deep shock, and then cried out in dismay, ''Oh, no, what happened to your hair?''

Farrah tells that story time and again to prove that her trademark hair style, which is as much a part of her image as that stunning smile, is not all God's creation. Rather, it exists with a little help from her hairdresser.

Actually to achieve that casually coiffed style, Farrah's hair is set on large rollers each morning at the studio. Since her tresses are layered, they go back in a wave when her hair is combed out. The rollers are set back and wind sideways toward the back of her head. She usually keeps the curlers in for about an hour, since her hair is full and thick and takes a long time to absorb the curl.

When Farrah first came to Hollywood, she wore her hair shoulder-length and cut all one length, and turned up in a flip. Her present hairstyle came about almost by accident.

"I wanted to grow my hair," she explains, "but as it became longer, it got thick. My hairdresser suggested the layering because of the weight problem, and before I knew it, I had a hairstyle that became identifiable with me."

Farrah is well aware that hordes of girls rush to their hairdressers carrying a picture of the blond angel and hoping that with a few snips of the scissors and a little time with some rollers, they will emerge looking like this dazzling star. But she cautions that it's not that easy. To achieve the look, which Farrah emphasizes is not a gypsy cut, the hair must be thick and full and rich. Brittle, thin, or fine hair just won't do. It helps to start with the kind of naturally fantastic and healthy mane that Farrah has.

The upkeep on this hairstyle is also time-consuming. You have to have the patience to work on it for about an hour, in between the setting, the blow-drying, the brush-out, etc. This style certainly does not fall into place. If it's not kept up, it tends to resemble a moth-eaten haystack. In short, it must be maintained or else it looks awful.

Part of the reason that Farrah has the kind of hair that

beauty salon artists love to get their hands on is that she takes good care of it. She washes it every single day, with a good shampoo, and follows the washing with a conditioner to prevent dryness. The streaking that her hairdresser does every four or five weeks also tends to dry her hair, so she uses a conditioner especially prepared for her, made from vitamins and oils.

Farrah also avoids the sun. She believes strongly that the sun is the worst thing in the world for your hair, and she always wears something on her head when she goes outdoors.

Her million-dollar hairdo is so well known and popular that many people simply call it The Farrah. It's the biggest celebrity style since Dorothy Hamill's wedge and Jackie O's puffy bouffant look from the sixties.

The genius behind the style is Allen Edwards, Farrah's ingenious hairdresser, and co-owner of the Jon Peters Salon in Beverly Hills.

"It's incredibly feminine and drives men crazy," Edwards declares, giving himself a well-deserved pat on the back for one of the most famous styles of the decade. "It's the ultimate in femininity, that's what I hear."

He describes it as a beveled haircut—it's one length in back, layered in angles at the sides—a sort of longer version of the shag, in vogue several years back.

How is it done? "Volume blowing, we call it," says Allen. "First with her head held down, I blow it out from the back with my hands going forward, lifting up the hose for volume. When it's 85 percent dry, I put all the ends into pincurls and attach them to the head so the ends have that flippy, feathery look. Then the pincurls dry and I blow it out again with my hands.''

The major consideration, of course, is the cut and the texture of the hair. If that's right and the proper setting and drying is done, then *voilá*—the Farrah look!

Ironically, while other women are making mad dashes to beauty salons to achieve the Farrah do, the star herself is considering a change. After all, she explains, she's been wearing her hair this way for about three years and feels that she's ready for a new look.

''I get stopped about twenty times a day by women asking who cuts my hair. I see them everywhere. Now I'm ready for something different.''

Although it's definitely that hair that makes Farrah one of today's top sex symbols, there's more to her good looks than that. She has special makeup and a carefully thought-out beauty regimen that she follows religiously. She enhances her natural physical gifts with some good old-fashioned beauty care.

Farrah uses the Lazlo program for her skin—a carefully prepared system of products designed for her kind of complexion that includes oils, creams, and astringents. Her skin tends to be oily, so she shuns the creamy cleansers and lotions that women with dry skin use to de-grime their faces. Instead, she relies on a simple soap-and-water routine to wash away dirt and makeup. The soap and water leave her skin squeaky clean, a sensation that Farrah loves. She doesn't need any moisturizers or emollients, since she finds that after a few minutes of exercise and moving around on the set, her own natural facial oils get revved up on their own, without any artificial help.

When she's not on camera, Farrah stays away from the heavy makeup that is essential under studio lights. She tends to apply just a little blusher, to keep her skin clear and let her pores breathe. She also uses an astringent with no alcohol after she washes her face. Her skin is sensitive, so she's careful about it.

Farrah's not one to indulge in a lot of false equipment to achieve her beauty. Falls and other artificial props are not in her beauty kit. She doesn't use false eyelashes, even when she's acting, because she feels that they make "your own fall out." Instead she applies natural products, like vaseline, to her lashes and brows. She follows this routine every night before going to sleep and believes that this makes them healthy and shiny and stimulates the hair growth.

She's enthusiastic about the benefits of mascara—especially the lash-lengthening kind. Each morning as part of her makeup, she applies several coats of mascara to both her upper and lower lashes.

Farrah also accents her gray-green eyes with subtle colors of shadow—hues in blue and green. The bluish colors make her eyes look greener and the green tones bring out the gray flecks in her eyes.

When Farrah was younger, she worried about her oily complexion, knowing that oily skin during the teenage years can mean blemishes and other troubles. Now that she's approaching thirty, however, she appreciates the natural oil her skin produces. The oil helps to retard aging and prevent wrinkles and creases.

She's always passed up heavy, sticky, pore-clogging makeup and creams. The only makeup she uses for street wear is simply a light base coat, barely noticeable.

Her beauty program also extends to her nails. She prides herself on her long, tapered nails that are usually colored with a light polish. Each evening she generally removes her polish, and in the morning her nails are manicured again.

Despite her late-night cravings for junk food like Cheetos and chocholate chip cookies, Farrah is a wise eater. She keeps her five-foot-six-inch frame an even 110 pounds through eating in moderation and constant exercise.

"You can eat anything you want as long as you only eat a little of it," advises Farrah. "I really like pizza and spaghetti, but I eat only a little of it. Eating in moderation is the key to staying slim."

Farrah doesn't really have to worry about keeping her weight down, but she is careful that she gets her share of required protein daily and that she eats healthy foods. Before she starts her day, she mixes herself a nutritious breakfast drink with powdered protein in it. She feels that this gives her an extra energy boost, particularly because she wouldn't normally eat breakfast. But if she has this high-energy drink, she finds that she isn't starved by lunchtime.

At lunch she eats salads with a light, lemony dressing. For snacks she likes cheese. And for dinner she likes steak

—cooked medium rare. Or else some boneless chicken dipped in bread crumbs and sautéed. Fresh fruits and vegetables are also high on her list.

Of course, like everyone, there are no-no foods Farrah adores that aren't particularly good for her. She craves Coca-Cola by the quart, but always dilutes it with lots of ice to reduce the calories.

Farrah also believes in vitamins, especially vitamins A and D, because they help to improve her circulation. Since she's been involved with the long hours and heavy work load of a weekly series, Farrah finds that her body longs for the proper vitamin supply to keep her going. If she feels she isn't getting enough from her diet, she takes vitamin supplements.

Generally, however, she eats the kinds of foods that nutritionists recommend for staying healthy. Chicken, fresh vegetables and fruits, salads with lemon juice, cold drinks with lots and lots of ice to cut down on the calories.

Farrah also doesn't smoke, which is another plus for her complexion. She also rarely drinks, except for perhaps some wine with her dinner.

An athletic girl who slithers from golf course to tennis court, Farrah also believes in daily exercise to keep her svelte shape. No matter how much she's yawning in those early-morning hours before the studio limousine comes to pick her up, Farrah insists on carrying out her daily exercise regimen. This consists of a few deep knee bends and some other basic stretches before she toddles off to work. At night, she adheres to the same routine. No matter how tired, no matter how much she'd like to get a few extra minutes of shut-eye,

Farrah is disciplined enough to work out twice a day. That's what keeps her in such top-notch condition.

Farrah Fawcett, lion-maned goddess of beauty, may be one of the best-looking actresses ever to appear on the small screen. The teeth are perfect, the skin is peachy, the smile is incandescent, and the body is lean and curvy. But mostly it's the hair—that gorgeous, free-flowing head of hair that has become Farrah's trademark. Yes, Farrah is certainly beautiful, but in spite of it all, in spite the sacks upon sacks of fan mail, in spite of the adulation, Farrah's pretty philosophical about her looks. She can take them with a grain of salt.

Once an interviewer asked Farrah when she first realized she was beautiful. She thought for a minute, then flashed that glittering smile, and said merrily, ''Until the makeup man got here—until then it was touch and go!''

Cherish those moments when Farrah's gliding through "Charlie's Angels" or Lee's bounding bionically in "The Six Million Dollar Man." This golden duo have set their sights on movies and are hoping to seque from series fame to film stardom. This would undoubtedly mean farewell to their shows. "Charlie's Angels" would survive, with a suitably fetching replacement for Farrah, as blond and lithe as she is. But "The Six Million Dollar Man" would go off the air, if Lee should decide to leave the show.

With feature films in mind, Farrah and Lee have formed their own husband and wife production company. The name, appropriately enough, is Fawcett-Majors Productions, and they hope to create, through this joint venture, important movies, for release in both theaters and on television.

Lee has recently filmed a movie in Canada, to air on NBC

this fall, called *A Matter of Innocence*. Farrah is mulling over a number of projects. Among them are the starring role in the film versions of *The Fan Club* and also the screen adaptation of Rosemary Rogers' best-selling novel, *Sweet Savage Love*.

The name Farrah Fawcett-Majors might take up a lot of space on a movie marquee, but that hasn't diminished her desire to make it big on the silver screen. Farrah thinks she has movie star potential and so does her husband. As a matter of fact, she has had some forty-two offers for roles in various movies. She may not be a whiz at higher math, but Farrah can figure out that if as many as ten million people are expected to buy her poster, that makes for a lot of box office appeal. At three dollars a ticket, that comes to an astounding thirty million dollars' worth of box office potential.

"She does not need a pocket computer," says her manager Jay Bernstein, "to figure out how great her popularity might be."

Lee considers his blond wife a logical successor to screen star Marilyn Monroe, the one person who would rejuvenate movies with some good old-fashioned feminine appeal.

It would seem that Farrah could easily become the glamour girl of the seventies, taking up the legacy left by other movie queens like Elizabeth Taylor and Rita Hayworth. She's beautiful and appealing, yet all in a very innocent, girl-next-door sort of way. It's a rare blend.

But first Farrah wants to prove she can really act, and is not just a pretty showpiece for a movie set. She doesn't want to be just an attractive knickknack in a film. She complained about lines and stories in "Charlie's Angels" that made her appear "too silly" or "too giggly." She also objected when a scene called for her to wear a bikini when street dress would have made more sense. While Farrah admits that she has to go a long way before becoming a truly great actress, she also wants properties that will help her develop and grow.

"I'm certainly not a Faye Dunaway," she concedes. "There are certain parts I cannot do. But I'm learning all the time."

The parts that Farrah would like for herself are not all froth and whipped cream. She'd like real, meaty parts with drama and action. She doesn't want to be just a beauty queen. She would willingly go against character and break out of the mold she's previously been in. It would mean a startling change of pace for the Southern girl with so many old-fashioned values, but Farrah is confident she could handle the challenge.

She also expresses hope about playing a more grass-roots, down-to-earth kind of character. Perhaps a troubled house-wife or a frontier woman or a beleaguered businesswoman. Something like the nitty-gritty role that Faye Dunaway played in the movie *Oklahoma Crude* with George C. Scott, about hunting for oil.

She speaks of doing "a picture with real woman's emotions." Nothing along the lines of Lady Macbeth or Hamlet's Ophelia, but a character with more drama and poignancy than she's played before. Her role as the storm-tossed, calamity-stricken heroine in *Sweet Savage Love* may be just what she has in mind.

One facet of Farrah's talent that has been rarely demonstrated is her knack for comedy. She's got a flair for being funny that would make her a natural for lighthearted escape movies, modern-day Rock-Hudson-and-Doris-Day–type capers, where there are beautiful clothes, gorgeous sets, handsome men, and of course Farrah, the breathtaking star. "I'd like to do a movie, a romantic comedy, about a warm relationship," admits Farrah.

Yet, despite all the fanfare and the awesome predictions for her future, despite the multiple offers and contracts dangled before her like so many sugar plums on a tree, there are other things that Farrah could do besides acting. She could walk away from it all tomorrow, if it was important, and return to her art—her sculpting and her painting. Or perhaps have that million-dollar baby that she and Lee have been hoping and planning for since they were married.

"I don't want to lose my perspective," she says. "I know my limitations. This way I have the best of both worlds. But . . . I'm not going to worry. I've never not worked, but it wouldn't matter to me if I stopped. I have a fulfilled life just being Mrs. Lee Majors."

But her adoring public will not let her stop working. Already the Hollywood moguls are eagerly seeking a Farrah Fawcett lookalike—someone who closely resembles her in hair, face, voice. They predict that such an actress could make a fortune—almost as much as Farrah, the original, does.

Lee is also expanding his creative horizons. In addition to his bionic duties on the weekly series, he has starred in a number of made-for-TV movies. He also hopes to become more involved with the behind the scenes work in show business, like producing and directing.

Lee remembers, all too disconsolately, how he was offered a costarring role in a new film when he was doing ''The Big Valley'' series. He had to turn it down because it conflicted with his schedule. The film was to become a classic and make great stars of the actors who played in the lead roles. The name of the movie was *Midnight Cowboy,* starring Dustin Hoffman and Jon Voight.

That's the pitfall of having a commitment to a series—the restrictions it places on your time. But having that series, in which he has at last emerged as a full star, is very important to Lee.

Over the past few years, Lee has been busy integrating other work into his ''Six Million Dollar Man'' schedule. He varies his acting duties with some intense efforts at directing. He feels it's important for an actor on a long-running series to develop other areas of expertise—to understand other facets of putting a show together. It's a trend that has been taken up by other series actors, such as ''Little House on the Prairie'' star Michael Landon, who has also directed some of his own shows.

Last year Lee starred in the gripping story of Francis Gary Powers, the American pilot who was gunned down by the Russians during an intelligence-gathering flight in a U-2 plane over the Soviet Union. The incident, which became a *cause célèbre* during the 1960s, was known as the U-2 affair. Majors starred as Powers in a true dramatization that was based on the pilot's 1970 book, *Operation Overflight*. It was a role that was quite a departure from his usual TV fare, and Lee earned critical applause for his work.

Especially with his own production company, Lee hopes

to do more impressive projects like this. The new schedule at Universal, where "The Six Million Dollar Man" is shot, allows for more free time for the actor. Should Lee decide to continue his bionic role, he'll have a longer hiatus to concentrate on other things.

"It's a half-year business now, so far as television is concerned," he says. "That's good for me in a sense. I'd like to have a chance to do some theatrical movie features."

If both Lee and Farrah leave their shows, it won't be in search of more lucrative ventures. As it is, with the fees she's earned from commercials and from "Charlie's Angels" (where she made $5,000 per show for the first season), plus Lee's five-figure-a-week income for his bionic work, they are something akin to a six million dollar couple in real life. Lee alone still makes thousands of dollars a year from residuals on "The Big Valley" and "Owen Marshall." Neither of them is hard-pressed for extra cash. They both want to do other things, especially projects that they can work on together and that get them away from the arduous routine of a weekly series.

Yet, however lofty their goals may be, both Lee and Farrah can hardly believe their success stories. "It happened so fast and so good for me, I still can't believe it," admits Lee. "It seems like just yesterday I was a fan of Steve McQueen's." These days Lee and Steve wind up at the same parties.

Some things will never be the same again. Farrah Fawcett will never again be just the wife of actor Lee Majors. The sky's the limit for this heavenly creature. As for Lee, well, he'll never have to work again in the parks department for a meager $2.83 an hour. After all, now he's a real six million dollar man with an angel of a wife!